IVEY BADGE 44

BY

JIM NORTON

Copyright © 2025 by Jim Norton
All right reserved.
This book is a production of Gold Badge Writing.
Janine Chellington Press | Central Kansas.
ISBN:979-8-9920026-0-7
LCCN: 2025900732

No part of this publication may be reproduced, copied, stored, or transmitted in any form or by any means electronic, mechanical, scanned, photocopied or otherwise without the express written permission from the publisher. It is unlawful to copy or post any portion onto a website or other means of display, without permission from Janine Chellington Press.

DISCLAIMER

Disclaimer; Use of names, Graphical Content and Ethical Considerations. This book employs real names, locations and entities unless explicitly stated otherwise. Any name changes will be noted. Some information or details depicted within could not be confirmed by more than a single source verification process.

Readers are advised that this narrative contains graphic descriptions of real-life incidents reflective of the challenges and realities law enforcement face. These depictions are intended to reflect an accurate and authentic portrayal of the experiences encountered in the line of duty. However, the author acknowledges the potential emotional impact of such content and urges readers to exercise discretion and self-care while dealing with these narratives.

It is crucial to emphasize the author does not share personal anecdotes of stories that compromise the confidentiality of operational procedures, trade secrets or sensitive law enforcement methodologies. This deliberate omission underscored the authors commitment to uphold the ethical standards of law enforcement practices.

Additionally, for persons named within this story, the author has sought and obtained permission from the individuals involved. The author's dedication to respecting the privacy and rights of those mentioned within these pages reinforces the integrity of the storytelling process.

Furthermore, this book does not intend to glorify or promote illegal or unethical activities. The intention is to present a balanced and honest account of real-life experiences while respecting storytelling's legal and ethical boundaries.

By choosing to read this book, readers acknowledge and accept these disclaimers, with the understanding the narratives depict a multifaceted nature and intent.

DEDICATION

This book is dedicated to the memory of Salina, Kansas, Police Officer Jerry R. Ivey, Badge Number 44. Jerry gave his life to protect the citizens of Salina, Kansas.

This book will take you beyond a journey where a hardened criminal crossed paths with a Police Officer, who on Friday, June 13th, 1975, became a hero.

I hope this historical journey enlightens people and brings peace, understanding and an informative look at what happens when a Police Officer gives all in the line of duty.

JERRY R. IVEY BADGE #44
END OF WATCH 06-13-1975
MAY YOU REST IN PEACE.

FROM THE AUTHOR

This is a true story. Some names were omitted while telling this story to protect those victims who were minors or severely traumatized by being victimized. Information used in writing this story was obtained using newspaper articles, court records, police reports, private interviews with people present during the events, and through open public records.

Nothing written within is meant or implied as anything other than facts for this book. Nothing written within is meant to cause pain or anguish to anyone living or related to persons named in this story.

The story is a heart wrenching tale of a man, a woman, three children, and friends who had to endure a sorrow that should never have been, along with a second family senselessly traumatized and victimized.

I wish to simply write the story to honor a man who I consider a hero. Nothing more or less than that. Jerry Ivey's story needed to be told.

Thank you for reading my book and understanding what occurs when a Police Officer gives all in the line of duty.

Jim Norton
Gold Badge Writing

TABLE OF CONTENTS

1. THE BEGINNING 1
2. IN THE ARMY NOW 5
3. FAMILY MAN 13
4. SALINA POLICE DEPARTMENT 19
5. SCHULTZ 27
6. SOMETHINGS NEVER CHANGE 37
7. ARRIVING ON THE DOOR STEP 41
8. THE ROBBERY 47
9. NO MAN'S LAND 53
10. A VIEW FROM A WITNESS 61
11. THE ARREST 65
12. AN UNFAIR AFTERMATH 73
13. THE OUTPOURING OF GRIEF 77
14. THE TRIAL OF ROY SCHULTZ 83
15. THE PRISON BREAK & WOODY'S ANGRY RANT 91
16. REPEATING FAILURES 99
17. TRIAL NUMBER TWO 107
18. THE PARK 111

SPECIAL THANKS & REFERENCES 117
LAST WORDS FROM THE AUTHOR 120
ABOUT THE AUTHOR, JIM NORTON 121

CHAPTER 1

I WANT TO TELL YOU A STORY.
IT'S A STORY ABOUT A GUY NAMED JERRY IVEY.
A TRUE STORY, I THINK EVERYONE SHOULD HEAR.
THIS IS JERRY'S STORY. SO, HERE YOU GO.

The Beginning

Summers were hot in Jerry Ivey's hometown of Gastonia, North Carolina. When rains finally arrived in September, the season changed from a blistering summer to early autumn, when the colors became mesmerizingly bright as the trees changed into the hues of reds and oranges. The vines of ivy thinned to show the edges of the hillsides and tree trunks they had earlier enveloped. Tall trees, most older than the oldest residents, were everywhere in the city. Most were southern yellow pines. Although, like most American towns, as many as a hundred different varieties of tree could be seen on any given day across this beautiful old city. One thing which sets Gastonia apart from other areas of the country is the height of their southern yellow pines and how thick the ivy grew.

Families in Gastonia embraced hard work and routine. Fathers labored in the mills, while mothers managed the household, ensuring everything ran smoothly. Children attended school, moving through their days with a sense of belonging that tied them to their town. Gastonia was a place where childhood unfolded naturally, like ivy climbing steadily upward, unnoticed but persistent. Kids walked to school, or, if fortunate, caught a ride on the bus. The trees and ivy that flourished throughout the town blended seamlessly into the background, their quiet presence paralleling the steady, unnoticed growth of the children themselves—rooted, reaching, and thriving without fanfare.

In 1964, Gastonia stood as a semi-famous textile city, shaped by its manufacturing roots. Unions and factories dominated the workforce, fueling southern economies. For many working families, livelihoods depended on these jobs. Yet, starting in the 1930s and continuing for decades, the steady shutdown of textile plants brought heartache and financial hardship to Gastonia's people. The closures by Parkdale Mills nearly devastated the city. Still, resilience prevailed. Companies like Wix Filtration, Freightliner Trucks, and Stabilus stepped in, keeping the local economy alive. Gastonia fought to survive, and even today, its trees and crawling ivy stand as quiet witnesses to its enduring spirit.

The Ivey family name has long been a standing fixture in Gastonia. By the 1960s, there were Ivey siblings, cousins, aunts, and uncles all over Gaston County—their family tree branches grew. Of these Ivey families, Howard and Eunice Ivey's homestead had been established just off Ivey Road on the outskirts of town. Several acres and a small pond made a great location for a childhood.

Howard and Eunice's children, Gene, Jerry, Mike, Don, Ron and sister Deloris began their education at Ryan Elementary. Each moving on to Hunter Huss High School, named after one of the first school superintendent's W. Hunter Huss. The high school sits on a fifty-two-acre tract of land, outlined by huge pine trees on three sides. A forest of trees also floods the surrounding neighborhoods in the heart of Gastonia. Famous alumni who have walked the halls include Fred Durst of the band Limp Bizkit and NBA players Bubba Wilson, Hassan Whiteside, and Kris Lang, to name a few.

Howard and Eunice were proud of each of their children—their son Jerry was no exception. Success would follow him, however, a conventional route was not in Jerry's playbook. In 1964, an inner pulling took hold of Jerry wishing to see the world and he knew the draft would soon call him forward so he decided to enlist instead. With guidance from Eunice and Howard, Jerry decided to drop out of high school, get his GED, and join the Army.

As with all mothers, Eunice did not want Jerry to take this route in life; however, like most mothers who wish the best for their children, she understood where Jerry's heart and dreams where as he no longer wanted life in Gastonia. It was time for him to fly.

After a long talk with his parents, his mom agreed to sign the entry form for her seventeen-year-old kid to join the Army. In no time at all, Jerry shook the hands of his father and brothers, gave his mom a kiss, hugged his sister, and off to boot camp he went. Jerry was a kid, leaving Gastonia and a man entering the world. That is how adult life started for Jerry Ivey. The rest of his journey would be written over the next ten years.

.

JIM NORTON

CHAPTER 2
In The Army Now

All he wanted was to see the world. What better way than to join the Army? So, after getting beyond the issue of parental approval, off he went. It was July 23, 1965, when the Ivey's dropped their son off so he could see the world. He was a 135-pound kid when he stepped off the army boot camp bus and put feet on the ground at Fort Jackson, South Carolina. Jerry was about to find out what boot camp challenges lay ahead and he was excited about it.

Like all PFC's, Jerry ran mile after mile, climbed ropes, learned how to march in formation, ran some more, and shot rifles. The army taught him how to quickly fall sleep, and how to shower in less than three minutes. Calories burned off him from the exertion of boot camp. Jerry, like others before him survived the rigors of boot camp, however after the eight-week training, he was ready to start his military mission.

After boot camp, Jerry went to Fort Knox, Kentucky, for a training course. Jerry was going to be an Army cook. While at Fort Knox, Jerry completed several culinary courses, and he became part of a large mess hall crew, responsible for feeding thousands of soldiers. The Fort Knox experience lasted from September through early December, 1965. Jerry's world travels were about to begin. His orders had come down and he was going to Germany. Having never traveled far from the Ivey stomping grounds in North Carolina—Germany looked like a great place to start his military journey abroad. The Germany tour began on December 17, 1965. Being sent to Germany would also keep him from actually having to fight in Vietnam. Even though he never fought in Vietnam, Jerry provided invaluable support services to other soldiers, and he would always be listed as serving during the conflict.

Jerry rose through the ranks from E-1 to E-4 in Germany, within the first eight months. His tour in Germany ended the first week of September, 1966. During the latter portion of his Germany deployment, the command staff promoted him from an E-4 to a SP-5, or Specialist-5. He was given a pass to return to US soil to complete his service state side. Jerry's final military assignment was on the glorious Army base known as "The home of the Big Red One." Jerry was going to be stationed in Fort Riley, Kansas.

On September 6th, 1966, Jerry Ivey came home. Well, sort of home. He landed in Fort Riley, Kansas, where he was assigned to 387th Re-supply Company where he would continue his culinary duties as a cook and mess hall manager. Jerry was assigned to several different manager level duties while he served at Fort Riley, however they all had to do with support through the mess hall. His final duty, MOS [Military Occupational Specialty] assignment sent him to the 23rd Division of HHC/FASCOM [Headquarters and Headquarter Company / Field Army Support Command]. This was a support assignment that could send a soldier to many different assignments. Jerry's assignment was to the mess hall.

During his short two year stay at Fort Riley, his days off would often find him driving his car forty-five minutes to the west, so he could spend his off duty with his new sweetie. It all started one Saturday night in the fall of 1967 when Jerry and an Army buddy had decided "to cruise for chicks" on Santa Fe Street in Salina. Boys and girls had mastered the art of cruising main streets all over America and Salina, Kansas, was no different.

On a fall Saturday night while "Cruising Fe," Jerry Ivey and Maryann Burgess crossed paths and caught each other's eyes. It was an attraction at first sight and each, while in hunt for a partner had found what they had been looking for. Jerry had found his girl and Maryann had found her guy.

Over the next few months, when possible, Maryann drove to Fort Riley to spend time with Jerry. On one occasion, Maryann and her sister Linda Burgess, drove together to Fort Riley just so Maryann could see Jerry for an hour or two. Maryann's sister Linda remembered how Maryann was smitten over Jerry. Linda knew her sister had found "her guy" and thought it was fun to see how smitten Maryann had become. Both Jerry and Maryann had professed how they each wanted marriage.

However, before that could happen, Jerry had to survive HHC (Headquarters-Headquarters Company), a support division responsible for handling support to all operations within Fort Riley. The assignment was a stable position. Because of this assignment, Jerry had set duty hours like a civilian job and he considered his position as more of a restaurant manager than anything else. By the time Jerry entered his third year of active duty, he had settled in, and had proven he was dependable until April 7, 1968, when he was not.

Jerry was well known and liked by his commanders at Fort Riley. He had never been in trouble or given the commanders reason to question his leadership abilities. Until he did. Jerry missed a roll call. Then he missed another. Two in a row. No one could reach him during those two days, and he was listed as being AWOL (Absent Without Leave). During his AWOL period, without notice or warning, he showed back up on base at 0400, April 9, 1968. His commander was Colonel Eugene Seaburn, and he was not impressed nor happy about Jerry going AWOL. However, Jerry was lucky. Colonel Seaburn was both calm and a man of integrity, and he knew Jerry as being a dependable soldier. He was only twenty-two years old, and Colonel Seaburn figured there was a problem and he believed he knew what the problem was, he just did not know her name. After getting a next-level ass-chewing, Jerry confessed and told Colonel Seaburn her name. It was Maryann.

Instead of getting any time in the brig or major punishment, Colonel Seaburn issued an article 86 code violation, which cost Jerry one rank and $50 pay for one month. If he kept his nose clean until his end of service date, he could regain the rank of SP-5 and the weekend with Maryann would only cost him $50 pay. He accepted the punishment and did not break the rules again. Finally, after turning in all his gear, checking all the necessary boxes, Jerry's military service came to an end on August 1st, 1968. He would marry Maryann on August 2, 1968.

Jerry Ivey and Maryann Burgess were wed at St. Mary Queen of the Universe Church, Salina, Kansas. Photograph in Salina Journal, August 8, 1968.

The wedding was attended by all of Maryann's family and friends as well as a few of Jerry's family. After a short honeymoon back in his home state of North Carolina to show off his bride and introduce her to his family, Jerry would make Salina, Kansas, his new home.

Maryann's family was a staple in the Salina community as they were business owners. Maryann was not leaving Salina, which meant Salina was getting a new permanent resident. The entire Burgess family, especially Linda Burgess, saw how well Jerry and Maryann fit together and how Jerry's infectious personality made her family fall in love with him. Linda considered Jerry a brother. She could be heard saying Jerry was fantastic. She was not alone with these feelings. Jerry was simply a likable guy.

IVEY BADGE 44

Many Army soldiers, from all around this great nation have spent time at Fort Riley, Kansas. Every now and then, one of those soldiers remains in Kansas. Jerry signed up for it through marriage. A life in the great State of Kansas lay ahead of him.

As Jerry arrived in Salina and got settled in, he went to work for Maryann's family business, Burgess Schwinn Cyclery. Jerry worked in the shop building brand new bicycles, repairing broken ones, and learning how the business worked. He was a good mechanic. He had learned his mechanical skills growing up in a large family and he enjoyed working on mechanical issues and building things. After the wedding, Jerry settled in and began feeling at home in Salina. It was easy for him to make friends as he had charisma.

While working at the bicycle shop, he met a man named Bruce Sikora. Bruce was a sales representative for the Schwinn Bicycle Company. Bruce would make stops along his sales route and one of the stops was Burgess Schwinn Cyclery. During one of those distributor stops, Jerry and Bruce met and became instant friends. The friendship was more than a salesman/distributor association. The guys became really good friends. It was because of their similar personalities, that made them feel like brothers.

Linda Burgess reflected that during one of the stops while checking in on his bicycle distributors, Jerry and Bruce began chatting about life and Jerry asked Bruce if he was seeing any girls or if he was looking for a good gal to date. After some deep conversation on the subject, Jerry arranged for his sister-in-law, Linda Burgess to meet Bruce. Match making was not Jerry's forte, however within a few months, and after another wedding, Bruce and Jerry became brothers-in-law.

Like most young newlyweds, Jerry and Maryann endured a short stay at a tiny rented apartment; however, within a year, they moved into a bigger duplex as a married couple. Their duplex was located on Anderson Street. Married life was becoming normal and routine and Maryann was showing off her husband to all of her friends. After being married for about eighteen months, in June, 1970, Maryann held a bridal shower at their house on Anderson Street, for a close friend. Jerry and Maryann were well on their way to becoming a permanent fixture in their Salina Community. Life for them was getting great.

Jerry also knew he wanted more from life, at least in the realm of a career. He knew deep down his real desire was to become a police officer. This idea had been planted in him by his friend, Jim Huff. Jim had been an officer with the Salina Police Department for six years and Jim had been friends with Maryann for more years than that. It took Jim almost no time to convince Jerry he would make a good police officer. Jerry believed being a police officer would open many doors for the pair.

This new position promised a bigger paycheck and health insurance—essential as they planned to start a family. Jerry drove to City Hall, found the personnel office, and picked up an employment packet outlining the city's benefits. Nervously, he filled out the application to become a police officer for the Salina Police Department—and then he waited.

On June 16, 1970, after completing a rigorous hiring process that included a written test (which he passed), an interview with staff, and a psychological evaluation, Jerry faced one final challenge: a formal interview with Chief John Woody. Within twenty-four hours, he was officially hired as a police officer for the Salina Police Department.

What Jerry did not realize during his interview with Chief Woody was that he already had an advantage in the hiring process. Chief Woody, well-connected and familiar with nearly everyone, happened

IVEY BADGE 44

to be a personal friend of Maryann's father, John Burgess. As the saying goes, knowing the right people never hurts. In fact, Chief Woody had begun his storied career in Salina in 1959.

At just twenty-two years old, Jerry quickly found his place among his fellow officers in blue. He was soon outfitted with both summer and winter uniforms, black boots, a gun belt, a Model 15 Smith & Wesson revolver, pouches for extra bullets, handcuffs, a nightstick ring, and a duty hat tailored to fit perfectly. He also received two badges—one for his uniform shirt and one for his hat. The hat badge proudly displayed the number 44, marking the moment "Badge 44" became Jerry Ivey's official identifier.

Within months of settling in Salina, Jerry fell in love with his new town. It was the perfect fit for he and Maryann—a place that felt like home. Salina, Kansas, USA.

JIM NORTON

CHAPTER 3

Family Man

Officers hired in the sixties and seventies were not rushed off to training academies as they are today. Young officers were shown the ropes by way of an experienced training officer. They rode shotgun for weeks or months, depending on whether they had previous experience and how well they perform under pressure. During his time as a rookie, Jerry was assigned to veteran Police Officer Marvin Pratt. Jerry rode shotgun watching Marvin work and loved every second of it. Marvin could see Jerry was intelligent, hardworking and down to earth. Marvin could see he had the qualities it took to be a good cop.

During Jerry's rookie months he learned the street names of his new town. He understood how addresses flowed from north to south and east to west. He was shown the way reports were expected to be written and how policies were expected to be followed. Jerry probably found this rookie period, like so many before and those who followed after, to be the best period in any officer's career.

Being a rookie is great, because everything is new and exciting. As with all rookies, they are expected to make mistakes and learn from those mistakes. Although Jerry was not from Salina, he proved to be a pretty quick study for a rookie. He was bright and willing to learn. He listened and observed experienced officers. He took being a police officer seriously, however policing was not his entire life. He was a married man, who planned on raising a family with the love of his life.

Within just a few short years, Jerry would go from a Patrolman to a hero. The transformation would take only a matter of seconds. But let's not jump ahead. You should enjoy his journey leading up to becoming a hero.

In 1970, at the start of Jerry's career, he and Maryann were ready to start their family. They both were raised in large families and both had lived childhoods where all corners of their families were involved in their daily lives. The Ivey family had brothers, the Burgess family had sisters—Jerry's in North Carolina, Maryann's were in Kansas. Everyone knows kids keep their parents busy and are the center of their attention and lives. Jerry and Maryann wanted that. They were ready to start their perfect family.

Jerry loved his role as a police officer. Daily as he put on a freshly pressed dark blue uniform, pinned his badge and name plate on his chest, making sure his boots were shined, he displayed his pride for the job to everyone who knew him. Jerry took the position of Police Officer seriously and wanted to leave a good impression with citizens. His friends like Jim Huff, Ron Styles and Bill Pettijohn always enjoyed being around him. Jerry also felt a contentment every time he walked into the police station, even on the night shift where he had not gotten enough sleep before going to work. He was proud to have joined the men in blue of the Salina Police Department (SPD). But even more, he loved this family. Jerry had the perfect setup. A loving wife and a great job with a steady income and retirement. Jerry was a happy guy and everyone around him could see how he felt inside.

His friendly personality and easy going style were easy to enjoy. "It was infectious," Linda Burgess described. Along with Linda, her mom Marie, and sisters, Joanie and Debbie, each could see the love between Jerry and Maryann.

Two other people who were fond of young Officer Jerry Ivey were Darrell and Carol Wilson. Darrell had been the Assistant Chief of Police for years, and was involved in the hiring process of new officers. Darrell's wife, Carol described a time when Jerry arrived at their house on Oakdale Street to fix a bicycle for her. Carol was having trouble with a bicycle she really enjoyed riding and had asked if Jerry could help her fix the chain. As Carol fixed a pitcher of iced tea. Jerry went to work fixing the bicycle. They sat on the Wilson's large front porch of the old red Victorian home, drank tea, and talked while Jerry worked on a bicycle. Jerry turning the wrenches until the bike was in top working order. Carol said she was so proud of Jerry, as he was so willing to make peoples days better. A smile lit up her face while talking about Jerry.

Jerry also spent time showing the kids in the SPD youth baseball league how to properly field a baseball and how fundamentals helped them while playing the game. He enjoyed coaching little league baseball and loved working on neighborhood kids' bicycles when a kid needed a chain fixed or hand bars adjusted. An image of Jerry is what should pop into your mind when you imagine "a nice person." Giving people the respect he hoped they would give him back, that was his trademark—his calling card. Little did Salina know how lucky they were to have a person like Jerry Ivey.

As Jerry and Maryann settled into their first marital home at 515 Anderson, it did not take long before they were expecting child number one. On a hot July day, as Maryann's pregnancy came full circle, Jerry and Maryann waiting in the birthing room at the Asbury Hospital to welcome their first born into the world. A son, they would name John Scott Ivey, soon showed up and made his grand entrance. It was July 2nd, 1971. The little boy would be known to family and friends as Scott. Like all new mothers, Scott became Maryann's world. Motherhood fit her like a well-tailored dress, Linda would later say, when thinking back about her sister. Linda said Maryann took to motherhood like a duck to water. Maryann had a lot of support to help her during the early days of the first child. Her mother and sisters were always there for her, as was Jerry.

In true Jerry Ivey fashion, he took his responsibly as a father seriously. He constantly held baby Scott, helping with diapers, feeding, and bedtime duties. Jerry and this little boy were growing a bond that would not be broken.

Then, in the middle of the night during a cold January winter, about six months after Scott was born, the child became very ill. Scott developed a high fever and was admitted into the Asbury hospital. Both Jerry and Maryann were fearful of what had made their son sick. The doctors could never be sure, however they believed the illness showed all the telltale signs of spinal meningitis. Although Scott would survive the illness, the sickness left him disabled.

After returning home from the hospital, Scott had a seizure. As the seizure subsided, baby Scott showed signs of a severe disability with his vision. Whatever the illness had been, it also impaired his mental acuity. After the illness had passed and Scott became disabled, the bond between baby Scott and Jerry became even stronger. The little boy would always want to be held by his dad and would attach himself to Jerry whenever Jerry was home. Jerry spent all the off duty time he could with Scott, and the two became inseparable.

Even with the difficulties of dealing with a handicapped child, Jerry and Maryann decided to add to their family. Both knew the duplex on Anderson Street could not be their family's landing spot. It simply was not big enough and it simply was not their forever home. After going to the bank to secure the credit needed for a mortgage, the house hunt heated up. After many open houses, they found the house they wanted to turn into a home. On December 14, 1971, Jerry and Maryann became the proud owners of their family home at 725 Washington Street.

Maryann and her sisters had grown up just three blocks to the east of 725 Washington Street. The Ivey's new family home was a small, cute three-bedroom house on a large corner lot with plenty of room for growing kids to build forts and entertain their friends. Life for the

Ivey family was starting to get good.

In 1973, a second son who they named Anthony Jered Ivey entered the world and joined the family. This little boy would forever be called Tony. Almost one year later, in 1974, the Ivey family was fully set, as the third son, Jerry R. Ivey II was born, bringing the family count to five.

By the time 1974 had rolled around, Jerry and Maryann and the boys had settled into their permanent home. The house had a small garage along the east side, where Maryann parked the family car after running errands or visiting friends. The front door of the home opens onto a small front porch, which was always welcoming. It is a cute, small home that would be filled with love. Jerry, Maryann, and the kids were a young family as typical as a family could be.

The Ivey family home, 725 Washington Street, Salina, Kansas. Photograph taken by author, 2024.

The Ivey family lived just as most families in Salina live. Quiet, yet engaged. The boys ran around the house making messes and being noisy as little boys do. Mom and Dad showed equal love to each of them. They were not rich, but wealth can be determined in a number of ways. The Ivey family had the wealth of togetherness and love and everyone who knew the family could see it.

Jerry Ivey and the three boys. John Scott in Jerry's right arm, Jerry II is on his lap and Tony is on the couch behind his father. Taken the day prior to Jerry's death. Photo Courtesy of Jerry Ivey II.

CHAPTER 4
Salina Police Department

In 1970, Jerry began his journey with the Salina Police Department (SPD). He was assigned to a shift by Patrol Division Captain Ken Brown. The officers were assigned to work month long shifts leaving the midnight officer's sleep deprived. Having to attend court after working a long shift, or going to training after their shift. Jerry powered through the tough work schedule and helped raise his family with his wife. Life seemed hard for Jerry at times as it did on all young officers, however, through all the long shifts, which left him feeling worn out, he loved every minute of it.

In 1970, the SPD did not rush new officers directly into the police academy. The department wanted the young rookies to learn and see what being a cop was actually like, before sending them to the Kansas Law Enforcement Training Center (KLETC). It was during 1970, while a recruit in training that Jerry was assigned to Field Training Officer (FTO)Marvin Pratt. Officer Pratt was responsible for teaching Jerry every facet of being a cop. He often quizzed Jerry on how the street addresses were assigned, how to properly write a report and how to deal with people during stressful calls. Pratt taught Jerry the phonetic alphabet so he could properly run a police radio, as well as how to safely conduct traffic stops. Another important duty Jerry learned during his field training was how to respond to bank and business robberies and what your responsibilities were for each. One of those duties was how to set a roadblock when needed. "Setting a roadblock" was simply a term used when robbery reports were dispatched. The officers did not physically block the roadways, they would rush to a location and strategically park in a position, which gave them a full 360 degree view of a thoroughfare, so they could monitor traffic and locate a suspect or vehicle much easier. Depending on how Jerry was absorbing the knowledge taught by Officer Pratt, would determine how long he would be assigned to the field training program.

Typically, a new recruit works at least one or two twenty-eight-day monthly schedules to get exposure to different types of calls during different hours of the day. Because of this, Jerry found just how much different calls for service on day shift were from calls on the midnight shift. Day shift officers were more exposed to a larger population of citizens. There are far more people out and about in the daylight. Night shift often turned into bar fights, or burglaries and drunk drivers. All the fun stuff happened after it got dark. Getting trained on all different type of calls was the goal the SPD had for their rookies.

While in training, on Wednesday morning, July 22, 1970, just after midnight, Jerry and Officer Pratt were inside conducting a bar check at the Red Pussy Cat Tavern on West South Street. While inside the tavern, someone threw a rock at Jerry's patrol car, cracking the windshield. Although not uncommon, this incident afforded Jerry the opportunity to write a damage to property report in furtherance of his field training. It also pissed Jerry off. Cops hate being disrespected. Jerry felt this was an act of disrespect toward himself, Officer Pratt, and the SPD as a whole. That's just how most cops think and feel and Jerry was no different.

As Jerry's experiences as a patrolman continued growing, he had to face the fact he would need to attend and graduate the police academy if he were going to be a certified police officer. Few officers have ever looked forward to attending the police academy, simply because it takes you away from the job you just started enjoying. The academy would also take Jerry away from his family. However, on October 5th, 1970, Jerry headed to Yoder, Kansas, to attend the police academy.

KLETC had been established in 1968 by the state legislators, to ensure all Kansas police officers became fully trained and certified as officers. Upon arriving, Jerry checked in for his stay and was assigned a roommate, given a rule book, and settled in for the three-week academy.

After studying hard and passing all of his tests, Jerry met all the requirements for certification. On October 25, 1970, he graduated from the Kansas Law Enforcement Training Center along with his classmates in KLETC academy class number Eleven. Jerry was now a full-fledged certified Police Officer.

As a certified officer, Jerry was assigned to a shift once he returned from the academy. He started his career as a fully trained officer on Monday November 2nd, 1970. The next four and a half years would show just how good of an officer he would become.

ON PATROL

On April 15, 1973, while dealing with a local man, Jerry was put in a dangerous situation. Although not uncommon in law enforcement, he got his first taste of what it was like to have a gun pointed at you. It was an experience he would not soon forget. Jerry was about to become involved in his first hand to hand struggle with an armed suspect. It was documented in SPD report 73-1998. It happened like this. While Officer Jimmy Miller was patrolling in an unmarked detective's car east bound on Iron Avenue, he began following a 1962 Ford passenger car, which Miller believed was speeding. As Officer Miller pursued the speeder, he keyed up the radio and asked for a marked patrol car to assist him in making a traffic stop. Jerry Ivey heard the radio traffic and moved into position to make the traffic stop for Officer Miller. The suspect stopped at the traffic light at Iron and Ohio Streets, and as it did, Jerry pulled his patrol car behind the speeder and turned on his red lights.

The suspect quickly took off and turned his car into an alleyway behind a house on the east side of Ohio Street. The driver stopped suddenly and bailed from the car and began walking as fast as possible toward the back door of the house. Jerry ordered the man to stop and as he did, the suspect looked over his left shoulder and stated, "what the fuck for, Pig?" That would be the first sign of the trouble. As Jerry ran, catching up to the man, the suspect suddenly turned to his left, raising his right hand upward toward both Jerry and Officer Miller. The suspect was holding a small silver handgun and he pointed the handgun at Jerry's face.

Jerry rushed the man, pushing into the suspect as he ducked to his right and grabbed the suspect's right hand, forcing the small handgun from his grip. While at the same time, pinning the suspects arm against a tree. As Jerry did all of that, he drew his revolver and pointed it against the suspect's left ear. Both Jerry and Officer Miller were able to hold the suspect against a tree, where he was ultimately arrested and handcuffed. No shots were fired.

The suspect would later claim he had never intended to shoot either Jerry or Jimmy Miller. The suspect, claimed during a later interview he had been harassed by a Fort Riley soldier earlier in the evening, and was just nervous about being messed with. Although both Jerry and Jimmy Miller would later feel relieved neither had been shot, the suspect should have felt the exact same way. On May 1, 1973, the suspect was bound over on a felony count of aggravated assault against Jerry. On Tuesday, June 19th, 1973, the suspect took a plea deal and plead to Disorderly Conduct and Carrying a Concealed Weapon. Judge Morris Hoobler deferred the sentencing until the suspect completed a mental examination at the Topeka State Hospital. It is unknown what happened to the suspect after that.

As Jerry continued down his career path, he continued gaining valuable experience. Another newsworthy case involving Jerry occurred on Sunday, April 30, 1973, shortly after midnight. As Jerry was conducting a tavern check at a club called the Tiki Room Tavern, he parked his marked patrol car, locked the doors and went inside to conduct a tavern check. As Jerry walked the interior of the bar, he talked with staff and the drinking public. As this unfolded, an intoxicated man in the parking lot decided to go "dancing" all over Jerry's patrol car. Witnesses who identified the man told police the suspect was literally dancing and stomping all over the car. The car sustained enough damage to be considered a felony level violation. The hood, top and trunk had been badly dented and scratched and in several locations, caved in. The light bar had been kicked and the red globes of the light bar had been broken out and lay on the gravel parking lot. It took the Police Department eight hours to round up the suspect, but he was booked into jail for felony damage to property. The suspect was arraigned on Monday morning and held on a $1,000 bond.

As the days rolled on, valuable experiences continued piling up for Jerry. Reoccurring without the officer actually realizing the experience building within themselves. Experience is what changes a rookie into a veteran. Another example of Jerry working hard came on the early morning hours of Sunday, December 16, 1974. Jerry went back to the Red Pussy Cat Tavern after being dispatched to assist with a large fight taking place inside the bar. Bar fights were not an uncommon occurrence as all patrolmen dealt with these situations. However, dispatch told the responding officers that the fight was "out of control." Because of this, four officers were dispatched. Jerry and Officer Bill Pettijohn arrived first and went inside to see what was happening.

While inside, Jerry found nearly every patron engaged in hand to hand combat with another patron. The noise within the bar was deafening and no one even noticed the officer's presence through all the utter chaos. Men were squared up and punches were being thrown. Many landed, which only raised the tension inside. The volume of the yelling and madness was so ear shattering it kept dispatch from hearing any calls for help being broadcast by either Jerry or Bill Pettijohn. All dispatch heard was a keyed up mic, followed by screaming and sounds of shattered glass. Jerry called for more back up, however the third and fourth officers could not make out the request. They were on their way, but not soon enough as far as Jerry and Bill Pettijohn were concerned. Every police officer knows that when something like this (a true large scale riot) happens, everybody involved gets to go to jail. The hardest part is getting the suspect in handcuffs, while performing the double duty of controlling the arrestee while also guarding your own safety. Initially, Officer Pettijohn was able to handcuff one of the fighters and Jerry was able to do the same to another, all while punches continued landing and screaming continued around them. It was pure mayhem.

Jerry remained inside the tavern trying to break up fights and keeping the peace, all while his arrestee was standing next to him in handcuffs. As this occurred, Officer Pettijohn walked his first handcuffed suspect out to his patrol car. As the rowdy arrestee arrived at the patrol car, Officer Pettijohn sat the bad guy into his car and placed the seat belt on him. The problem with this was, in 1974, prisoners were transported in the front seat. SPD patrol cars did not have cages or dividers installed between the front and back seats. Once Officer Pettijohn got the suspect secured in a seat belt, Pettijohn returned inside to help Jerry arrest more people. As Officer Pettijohn and Jerry continued dealing with the rowdy crowd inside, the suspect in Officer Pettijohn's patrol car slid as far to his left as possible and managed to get his left foot over the center hump of the patrol car, where he keyed up the police radio using his foot.

The suspect, who was a bit intoxicated, decided calling his girlfriend a string of foul names over the airways was just what Salina needed to hear. It made him feel better. Apparently he blamed his girlfriend for the predicament he found himself in. The barrage of foulness he spewed went on for several minutes, clogging up the SPD radio band as Jerry and Bill Pettijohn continued dealing with the fight inside the bar. Finally, after the listening public was fully informed of how the suspect really felt about his girlfriend, a third officer arrived and was able to remove the suspects foot from the radio mic. Numerous patrons were eventually arrested and they all found themselves in handcuffs. The bar fight was calmed and eventually stopped. The tavern closed for the night, leaving the employees of the Red Pussy Cat Tavern to clean up a huge mess of over turned-tables, broken glass, and messy floors.

The *Salina Journal* headline mentioned a "melee." Everyone got a good laugh about it, at Officer Pettijohn and Jerry's expense.

IVEY BADGE 44

Although not uncommon, it is calls like this, which make officers become true partners and close friends. Jerry and Officer Pettijohn became close friends during their time on the SPD and that single call would be remembered by both.

As time went on, while Jerry continued working hard and having fun, a serious crime spree was occurring to the east in Junction City. Kansas. The date was December 29, 1974, when a man by the last name of Mason robbed a billiards parlor in Junction City. He also robbed two customers before fleeing. However before leaving, he kidnapped the business manager, taking her hostage. After forcing his female hostage to come with him, Mason fled and broke into a nearby home. While committing this crime, he took the home owner hostage at gun point as well. Mason tied both women's hands and feet with lamp cords ripped from the wall. He rummaged through the house for any valuables he could find. While this occurred, the women sat on the floor terrified by their captor.

Several hours into the ordeal, as time passed and Mason decided what his next move was going to be, the business manager worked hard to escape her bindings. She was able to escape and ran to a neighboring house where she reported the crimes to the Junction City police. Because of the business manager's escape, Mason would flee the home, keeping control of the homeowner as his hostage. A short time later, a "be on the lookout" (BOLO) was broadcast state wide. After Mason was identified as the suspect, it was ultimately believed by the police that Mason would head toward Salina, as he was listed as a Salina resident.

As the BOLO went out to all agencies, the Saline County Sheriff's Department along with the SPD activated roadblock procedures along all points leading into Salina. In the early morning hours of December 30, 1974, a Saline County Deputy spotted Mason and his hostage traveling west bound on Interstate 70. A short chase between the deputy and Mason's vehicle ensued and Mason exited the interstate at the 9th Street exit. As he did, he was heading straight toward Officer Jerry Ivey's road block position.

Jerry was able to force the suspects' vehicle into a ditch due to his roadblock position, stopping Mason from continuing into Salina from the off ramp. Mason crashed his car into the north ditch, disabling the vehicle. The hostage fled her captures vehicle and escaped into the ditch and away from danger. Jerry and other SPD officers were able to take Mason into custody, at gun point, without further force being used. At the scene, Jerry searched Mason's car and located stolen cash from the robberies and a gun used in the assaults.

This incident would continue to show how Jerry Ivey had become a seasoned, hardworking officer. Over the five years of Jerry's law enforcement career, he strove to be the best cop he could. He was well liked and respected by both the public and his fellow co-workers. He gained vast experience as a police officer and was on his way to a long and proud career.

However, on the morning of Friday, June 13, 1975, all of that changed. So who is the "monster" in this story you may ask? Was he really a monster, or is that being too harsh? His name was Roy Earl Schultz. He was born in 1934. At the time of this story in 1975, he was forty years old. He was raised in Illinois and he was not your typical criminal; he was so much worse.

Similarly, Jimmy Lee Smith and Gregory Powell, notorious for the Onion Field murder of Officer Ian Campbell, or maybe the infamous Clyde Barrow of the Bonnie and Clyde duo. Hardened criminals who committed murder whenever they felt it justified—this is what this criminal in this story is like. Roy Earl Schultz continually showed a lack of empathy, guilt or remorse for anything he ever did, to anyone during his crimes. It was always about him, and no one else mattered.

Throughout his life, Roy Schultz was never known to displayed any redeemable characteristics, and if there were any, they were far outweighed by the evil he did. He would later be thoroughly diagnosed by specialists. It is believed however; he would probably have been diagnosed with Anti-Social Personality Disorder. No medical records of finding from specialist's interviews were ever found or made available. If he had any charming or friendly behaviors, no one in Salina, Kansas, ever witnessed them. He was what he portrayed himself to be, a horrible person.

CHAPTER 5
Schultz

So what makes someone become a criminal? Is it a psychological issue? Is it born out of desire or possibly the will to survive? Is the need to commit crimes spurred by poor parenting, at a young age? It could be one or more of these issues. But, it is also known that true hardened criminals have no remorse for their victims or crimes, nor empathy for people in general. They commit their crimes in a similar fashion, time after time, without any remorse for whoever they hurt. Once they find what works for them, they stick with it. That described Roy Earl Schultz almost exactly. Over time, his habits would be revealed, over and over again. Although his first conviction would occur in 1953. Many more would follow.

As crimes go, Schultz began with low level felonies such as theft or assault and soon blossomed into committing violent felonies. Robbery and aggravated assault seemingly became his favorites. Almost all his crimes centered around the theft of either money, guns or vehicles. His life seemed to become one violent criminal act.

For example, on July 3rd, 1967, Roy Schultz and one of his accomplices, committed an armed robbery and aggravated battery against a man outside of Mt. Auburn between Springfield and Decatur, in central Illinois. Schultz had dreamed up a robbery scheme where he called a business and told the salesman he was a representative of a large oil company, who wished to lease several of the company's wells. Schultz talked the businessman into driving him and his accomplice to inspect several oil wells in the countryside outside of Decatur, Christian County, Illinois.

As the three men arrived at the oil field, Schultz assaulted the businessman by pulling a knife, threatening to kill him as they were confined within the cab of the man's pickup truck. Schultz and his accomplice robbed the man of $90 cash and a diamond ring. Schultz then ordered the victim out of the pickup and drove off in the stolen truck, leaving the victim standing in a field as the robbers sped away. Several days later, both Schultz and his accomplice would be arrested, after the victim identified the two criminals by looking at mugshot books for the investigators. Schultz and his accomplice were booked into the Christian County jail. Their bond was set at $50,000, which in 2024 would be approximately $471,000.

This robbery was Schultz's first documented robbery; however, he was far from done. On July 8, 1967, an attorney for Schultz requested a bond reduction for him. After this routine court procedure, the Christian County Judge reduced Schultz' bond from $50,000 to $35,000. Afterward, Schultz either paid a $3,500 cash retainer, or he signed an 'I owe you" to a local bonding company and was out of jail. Roy Schultz would later stand in front of the same judge and plea to lesser charges. Plea deals are done for a litany of reasons, which include prosecution witnesses not being prepared or possibly forgetting specific details of a crime, evidence, which is considered "questionable," or because the prosecutor's office and the courts are over booked and feel the need to move justice along more quickly. Whatever the reason, in this case Schultz received a twelve-month prison sentence at a low level work farm institution and the case was considered closed. Schultz was incarcerated for the full twelve-month prison term.

After spending his incarceration in the Illinois State Prison system, he was released from prison in the spring of 1969. Roy Schultz was placed on Illinois state parole, which he quickly violated after another arrest. It was the summer of 1969 and after release from prison, he wasted no time continuing his criminal ways.

In August, 1969, Schultz began a three county crime spree, which included committing a grocery store robbery, the theft of an automobile and two burglaries to private residences. He showed absolutely no remorse or fear of being caught. Through good police work by the investigators in the three counties, he was ultimately arrested and charged with crimes in all three counties, however his overall bond was only set at $25,000, and these crimes were apparently not reported to the state parole office. Schultz never returned for those court dates after posting this Illinois court bond.

To truly appreciate the level of criminal activity Roy Schultz was involved in, one simply must examine his documented criminal history. Keeping in mind that his criminal history is only a documentation of being caught. An example of Roy Earl Schultz's criminal history, documented in the United States, Department of Justice records, shows the path of destruction leading to his upcoming crimes in 1975.

JIM NORTON

ROY EARL SCHULTZ
FBI #: 10-108D

Every person who is convicted of a crime is assigned a number by the FBI. Schultz's FBI number was 10-108D.

Roy Earl Schultz after his arrest on June 13, 1975. Photograph courtesy of the Smoky Hill Museum. Salina Journal Collection, File Photo.

ROY EARL SCHULTZ CRIMINAL HISTORY

1. POLICE DEPARTMENT, SPRINGFIELD, ILLINOIS.
Roy Earl Schultz, prisoner number 12720, arrest date: 2-15-1953. Investigation for theft. This entry shows an arrest for theft, but no disposition.

2. POLICE DEPARTMENT, KIRKWOOD, MISSOURI.
Roy Earl Schultz prisoner number 5733, date of arrest: 10-1-1958. Charged with Auto Theft, Attempted Robbery, Carrying a Concealed Weapon. No prosecution on Attempted Robbery. Warrant issued on Auto Theft and Carrying Concealed Weapon charges.

3. POLICE DEPARTMENT, CLAYTON MISSOURI.
Roy Earl Schultz, prisoner number SO98I, date of arrest: 10-3-1958. Charged with Carrying a Concealed Weapon, Stealing over $50. No disposition shown.

4. ST. LOUIS COUNTY PD, CLAYTON, MISSOURI.
Roy Earl Schultz, prisoner number 2708, date of arrest 10-10-1958. Charged with Suspected Armed Hold up. Released for lack of evidence.

5. SHERIFF'S OFFICE, SPRINGFIELD, ILLINOIS.
Roy Earl Schultz, prisoner number R-1734, date of arrest: 2-12-1960. Charged with Purchasing and Forging U.S. Postal Money Order. No disposition is shown. (However for this crime he was sent to a federal facility in Arlington, Texas on 3-3-1960.) Once in federal custody, he was given booking number 36658. This entry is a booking transfer log in, showing Schultz as being in federal custody. On 3-28-1960, he pled to these charges and was sentenced to 2-years in a Federal prison.

6. US CORRECTIONAL INSTITUTE TEXARKANA, TEXAS.
Roy Earl Schultz prisoner number 11729-TT, arrest date: 4-8-1960. As a result of a federal investigation into forgery charges, they added the charges of Receiving and Concealing Stolen Postal Money Orders. This was part of his Federal charges and on 8-18-60, Schultz was transferred to the federal prison in Terre Haute, Indiana. Schultz would be sentenced to 1 year and 1 day for a single charge of Receiving and Concealing Stolen Postal Money Orders.

7. POLICE DEPARTMENT, CHICAGO, ILLINOIS.
Roy Earl Schultz, prisoner number 73905, date of arrest: 7-14-1964. Charged with Robbery. There is no disposition for this charge, nor does it show if he was ever charged with any parole violations for violating his earlier parole.

8. POLICE DEPARTMENT, SPRINGFIELD, ILLINOIS.
Roy Earl Schultz, prisoner number 12720, date of arrest: 10-10-1964. Charged with Armed Robbery, Possession of Dangerous Drugs and Resisting Arrest. On 10-12-64, Schultz was released by arresting officers and no disposition is listed for these charges.

9. POLICE DEPARTMENT, ST. JOSEPH MISSOURI.

Roy Earl Schultz prisoner number 16-054, date of arrest: 11-15-1964. Charged with Burglary, Possession of Burglary tools, and Tampering with a Motor Vehicle. On November 18, 1964, the federal government had seen and heard enough of Roy Schultz and he was charged through Federal Court for "The Dyer Act." This charge had been the result of the November 15th arrest in St. Joseph, Missouri. The Dyer Act was created in 1919, which makes it a federal offense to transport a stolen vehicle across state lines. Since Schultz had apparently taken the stolen vehicle from Missouri into either Illinois or Kansas, he caught this charge.

Schultz would be convicted of this Federal offense and received a three-year prison sentence. He was transferred to the Leavenworth Correctional Institute on 2-19-1965.

10. POLICE DEPARTMENT, SPRINGFIELD, ILLINOIS.

Roy Earl Schultz, prisoner number 12720, date of arrest: 7-3-1967. Charged with Armed Robbery. This charge was the first of two Armed Robbery charges Schultz was arrested for, which are documented below.

11. SHERIFF'S OFFICE, TAYLORVILLE, ILLINOIS.

Roy Earl Schultz, prison number 256, date of arrest: 7-5-1967. Charged with Armed Robbery and Aggravated Assault. These two arrests resulted in a Federal Parole violation being issued, to go along with the two new cases. He was held on detainer at the Terre Haute, Indiana, federal prison. On 8-20-1967, a federal court convicted him on a parole violation, where he was remanded at Terre Haute, Indiana. However, he would soon be released.

12. POLICE DEPARTMENT VANDALIA, ILLINOIS.

Roy Earl Schultz, prisoner number 75290, date of arrest: 2-20-1968. Charged with Theft and Burglary. Disposition upon conviction, one year and six months in the Illinois state penitentiary.

13. POLICE DEPARTMENT, SPRINGFIELD, ILLINOIS.

Roy Earl Schultz, prisoner number 4451, date of arrest: 9-9-1969. Charged with Auto Theft and Unlawful use of a weapon. No disposition is listed for these charges, however on the same day,

IVEY BADGE 44

Schultz was arrested in Oklahoma with the stolen vehicle, which is where the Springfield charges stemmed from.

14. POLICE DEPARTMENT, MUSKOGEE, OKLAHOMA.
Roy Earl Schultz, Prisoner number 13275, date of arrest: 9-25-1969. Charged with burglary in the 2nd degree and Possession of Marijuana. A second charge of Burglary was added on 10-10-1969.

15. ALCOHOL, TOBACCO AND FOREARMS, OKLAHOMA CITY, OKLAHOMA.
Roy Earl Schultz, prisoner number E-4843, date of arrest: 9-30-1969. Charged with a Violation of the Omnibus Crime Control and Safe Streets Act of 1968. This federal attachment was the result of Schultz stealing a vehicle in Springfield, Illinois and taking it across state lines to commit further crimes.

The Omibus Crime Control Act was implemented in 1968 and ultimately turned out to appear as nothing more than a feel good program, written and signed into law by Congress. It allowed federal agencies to more easily assist state and local law enforcement with grants, funding and tools to help fight crime. It did however, keep Schultz in prison for a short period of time.

16. POLICE DEPARTMENT, MCALESTER, OKLAHOMA.
Roy Schultz, prisoner number 80035, date of arrest: 2-26-1970. Charged with Burglary in the 2nd Degree. Schultz was convicted of this crime and sentenced to 2 to7 years in the Oklahoma State Penitentiary. He was released after serving 2 years, 6 months.

17. POLICE DEPARTMENT, ARDMORE, OKLAHOMA.
Roy E. Schultz, prisoner number 731173, date of arrest: 10-30-1973. Charged with Grand Larceny, Possession of a deadly weapon and Defrauding an In-Keeper. A parole violation was not placed on Schultz and he bonded out as if a first time arrestee.

18. POLICE DEPARTMENT, MUSKOGEE, OKLAHOMA.
Roy Earl Schultz, prisoner number 13275, date of arrest 11-2-1973. Charged with Interstate transportation of switch blade knives. Schultz would later be convicted and sentenced to one year in federal

prison, however he only served time until being released on 1-21-1974.

19. POLICE DEPARTMENT, SPRINGFIELD, ILLINOIS.
Roy Earl Schultz, prisoner number 12720, date of arrest 2-3-1974. Charged with Felony Theft. (Note-Schultz committed this crime and was arrested while out on parole from the Muskogee arrest.)

20. FEDERAL CORRECTIONS INSTITUTE, TEXARKANA, TEXAS.
On 5-21-74. Taken into custody for Interstate transport of switch blade knives. Schultz would be given a sentenced of one year in Federal custody.

21. MEDICAL CENTER FOR FEDERAL PRISONERS, SPRINGFIELD, ILLINOIS.
Roy Earl Schultz, prisoner number 21558-149, date of arrest: 6-5-1974. Prisoner in transit from Texarkana, Texas. Schultz remains in Springfield until his release on 1-3-1975.

22. POLICE DEPARTMENT, COLUMBUS, MISSOURI.
Roy E. Schultz, prisoner number #4741, date of arrest: 2-15-1975. Charged with Possession of Burglary tools. Bond posted, no court disposition.

It should be noted Roy Schultz was not incarcerated in jail or prison between 2-15-1975 and 3-28-1975. He was a free man, and on the early morning hours of 3-8-1975, Sangamon County, Illinois, Sheriff's Deputy William D. Simmons would be murdered as he sat in his patrol car while checking a disabled vehicle outside of Springfield, Illinois. Schultz resided in Sangamon county at the time of this murder and was considered a prime suspect.

23. POLICE DEPARTMENT, DES PERES, MISSOURI.
Roy Earl Schultz, prisoner number 75-0837, date of arrest: 3-28-1975. Charged with Carry Concealed Weapon, Possession of Burglary Tools, and being a Fugitive. No disposition is listed, however he would be charged the next day by the Clayton, Missouri, Police Department in Saint Louis County, Missouri. He was arrested after a warrant was issued. The warrant charged him for Carrying a

Concealed Weapon and a Drug violation. Schultz was held for this warrant.

24. SHERIFF'S OFFICE, SPRINGFIELD, ILLINOIS.
Roy Ear Schultz, prisoner number C21764, date of arrest: 4-18-1975. Violation of Anti-Trust Law Petition to increase bail.

There are no records indicating how long Schultz was incarcerated after his April, 18, 1975 arrest, however it is known he went on the run after being let out of jail. On June 9, 1975, Roy Earl Schultz was on the run and had arrived in Wichita, Kansas, about to continue his criminal ways. Schultz had decided to head west, away from Illinois and Missouri and decided on wreaking havoc in Kansas.

JIM NORTON

CHAPTER 6

Some Things Never Change

Roy Schultz had left his stomping grounds, which reached between Illinois and Kansas City, Missouri, and into central and southern Oklahoma. As Schultz ran from the warrants in Illinois, he was apparently looking for new hunting grounds. Zebras do not change their stripes, and Roy Schultz was not looking for an eight-to-five job. On or before Monday, June 9th, 1975, Schultz arrived in Wichita, Kansas. Almost immediately he rented a cheap motel room and got busy scoping out new people and places to rob. During the early evening hours of June 9, 1975, Schultz began casing grocery stores to target. Schultz drove around different areas of Wichita, checking out different grocery store locations, as well as drivable escape routes he could use during his crime spree. Schultz had found grocery stores to be an easy and profitable target for his crime. He had proven this numerous times.

Schultz had learned from previous experience, grocery stores had several advantages. The first reason he loved them was they were profitable and held a lot of cash on hand that was quickly accessible. The second reason was they were not banks, which involved federal agencies like the FBI, which imposed much longer prison sentences if caught.

On June 10, 1975, Schultz would commit the first of his Wichita armed robberies at a Dillon's grocery store, located in the center of the city. He suspected there would be no confrontation with the store employees, as earlier robberies he committed had proven. There would also be no armed security to stop him. Schultz was not doing his robberies on a whim. He did his homework the day or evening before to be prepared. Schultz visited the Dillon's store, acting as a customer the evening before so he could learn the store layout. He wanted to spend as little time on the task as possible. This meant the fewest steps and in the quickest manner as he could. During the first Wichita grocery robbery, Schultz parked near the stores entrance. He approached the cashier in the cash office, where he brandish a handgun, pointing it at her face as he ordered the clerk to hand over all the money from the cash drawers and safes.

The Dillon's robbery went down just like that. As smooth as butter and as quick as a thief in the night. One difference between this Dillon's robbery and previous robberies was Schultz had brought a sidekick with him and he had never employed mace spray as a weapon. During the Wichita robberies, he had an unknown white male accomplice who stood by the front doors holding the can of aerosol Mace, along with a handgun and Schultz, armed with just a handgun did the actual robbery.

Schultz was successful in stealing a large amount of money from Dillon's and he and his unknown accomplice fled the store and drove away in a stolen Plymouth Valiant. They had just become nearly $3,000.00 richer.

The next day, June 11, 1975, in the mid-morning hours, Roy Schultz and the unknown accomplice drove to the Safeway Grocery Store at 1512 South Woodlawn in east Wichita. The pair followed the same method that had worked so well the day before. As the unknown accomplice stood guard at the main entry, holding a can of Mace and a handgun, Schultz walked to the cashier's room, forced the door open, and assaulted the cashier by pointing his handgun at the clerks face. Schultz told the clerk he would kill her if she did not place all the money into a paper bag. The clerk, terrified for her life, did what she was told. After the robbery was completed, he and his accomplice escaped the store and fled in the stolen Plymouth Valiant. Presumably, after the robbery, Schultz drove his stolen Valiant to his motel room and hid out until he decided what his next move was going to be. Police never learned who the unknown accomplice was with Schultz during the Dillon's and Safeway robberies, however there is a very plausible theory as to who he was, and it would probably relate back to March 8th, 1975 in Sangamon County, Illinois.

Wichita, Kansas, had just experienced two grocery store robberies in two days and Schultz had gotten away with both. No one was chasing him or even knew who or where he was. He had money in his pocket and was on top of the world. Roy Schultz felt both invisible and invincible, however he knew it was time to leave Wichita and find another hunting spot.

JIM NORTON

CHAPTER 7
Arriving On The Doorstep

It is believed that sometime during the day of Thursday, June 12, 1975, Roy Schultz left Wichita, and drove north toward Salina. Salina had no idea what they were about to encounter.

After arriving, Schultz drove around Salina and he spotted his next robbery location. He knew an easy target when he saw one. Schultz then rented a room at the Holiday Inn, located at 453 South Broadway. He likely chilled out for a while. Why he decided to rob the Dillon's grocery store located in Sunset Plaza at 1201 West Crawford is not actually known. It was close to his motel. It had numerous exit points to flee. So, that would seem like a plausible reason. This Dillon's was in a sprawling shopping center with businesses along each side of the store. The store was exactly what Schultz preferred. However, before he did it, he still had work to do.

During the evening of June 12, 1975, Schultz drove to the store and parked in the parking lot among other vehicles so he would not stand out. He entered the store for the sole purpose of getting the floor plan and identifying the quickest path to the cashier's area. Apparently Schultz stood out while doing so. An employee would later confirm and identify Schultz as having entered the store during the evening of the 12th as he purchased some trash bags as his ruse. When interviewed later, the employee stated Schultz was out of place and acted suspicious. She described the incident by saying "he just didn't belong." The employee had not seen or noticed another man being with Schultz at the time. When Schultz went to bed the evening of June 12, 1975, it should have been the last night he ever slept as a free man. However, it would not be and he would later show society just how much havoc he would wreak on the peaceful communities he would visit.

On Friday, morning June 13th, 1975, Jerry Ivey was assigned to work one beat by his shift Supervisor, a Senior Police Officer, Don Flick. Officers were allowed to fill in as supervisors on Friday shifts, since the patrol division was short on Lieutenants.

At this time in Salina, the Salina Police Department (SPD) had divided into six beats. Each beat was assigned one patrolmen. If a shift had more than six officers on shift, the extra officers would patrol as "safety officers" and those officers were not limited to staying in any single beat.

The SPD organizes its patrol system into designated areas called "beats." Each beat is defined by specific streets that form its boundaries. These beats are numbered 901, 902, 903, 904, 905, and 906. Officers refer to their assigned area as "One Beat," "Two Beat," "Three Beat," and so on, depending on the beat number. Officers

Salina Police Department Beats
901: North of the Elm Street.
902 and 903: Divided by Santa Fe Street. These beats extend from Elm Street south to Crawford Street.
904 and 905: Divided by Santa Fe Street and extends from Crawford Street, south to Magnolia Street.
906: Encompasses everything south of Magnolia Street.

IVEY BADGE 44

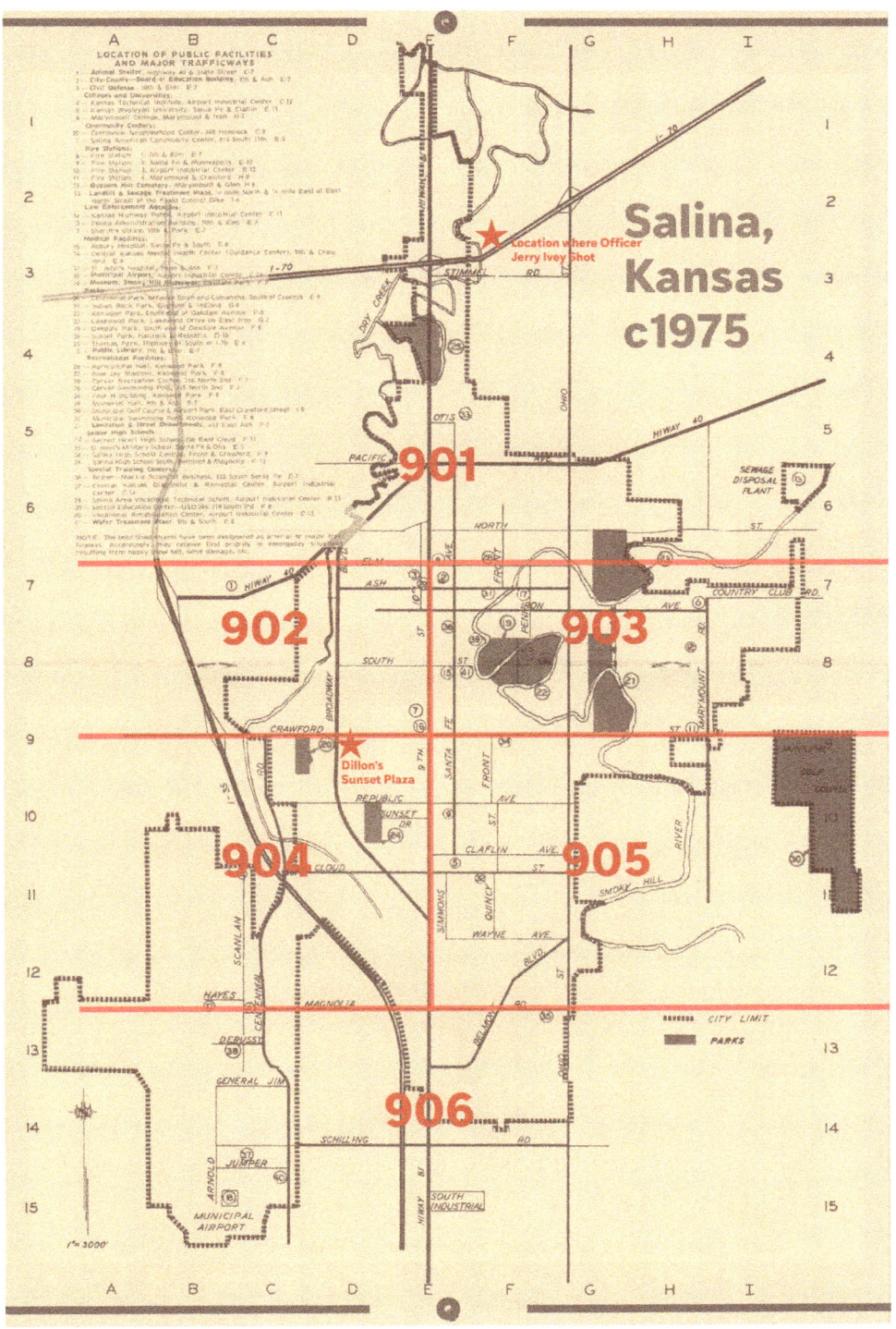

operating within a specific beat use the corresponding radio call sign, such as 901, 902, etc., and are expected to drive a patrol car marked with the same beat number, like Unit #901 or Unit #902.

The SPD divided the entire city's geographical footprint into six areas. Each area or beat, is designed to allow an officer to be able to run what is known as "code three" (lights and sirens) to attend to an emergency call, being able to arrive at a designated location in a four minute time period or less.

On Friday, morning June 13th, 1975, Jerry Ivey was assigned to work Salina's farthest north beat, known as beat 901 or One beat by his shift Supervisor. Each beat is assigned one patrolmen. If a shift had more than six officers on shift, the extra officers would patrol as "safety officers" and were those officers were not limited to staying in any single beat. The reason a Senior Patrol Officers assigned the beats on this morning is because the patrol division was short on Lieutenants and allowed the senior officer the experience of acting as a supervisor.

Normally, Jerry would have been assigned to work beat 903, or Three beat, as it was his normal work area. Because he was switched to work one beat, Jerry's radio call sign for the shift was 901. 901 was the north beat, which encompassed the area between Elm Street and Interstate 70 (I-70).

On any regular day in One beat, an officer could expect to work a vehicle accident or two, write a report for a theft and possibly write some traffic tickets to a speeder or stop sign runner. However, this day shift would be like no other day in the history of the Salina Police Department.

It had been thirty-three years since the SPD lost Officer Olney E. Eaton to an on duty death. That date had been May 21, 1942. Officer Eaton's death was due to an automobile accident and no one on the SPD had experienced what they were about to experience.

Around 7:00 am, as day shift officers were beginning their shifts, stopping by convenience stores loading up on coffee and reading over the briefing "hot sheets" as officers did, Roy Schultz was waking up and getting ready to go to his job. The job he was going to was called Dillon's Sunset.

At the same time Jerry Ivey was beginning his shift patrolling beat 901, his wife, Maryann Ivey was waking their three little boys, getting them breakfast, dressed and ready for their day. The children were not old enough to be in school, besides it was mid-June and school was not in session. Maryann had planned on taking the boys with her as she did the family's weekly grocery shopping at the Dillon's Store nearest to their home. That Dillon's store happened to be Dillon's Sunset, located at 1201 West Crawford Street. The time was approximately 8:00 am.

JIM NORTON

CHAPTER 8

The Robbery

It had been just after 6:30 am when Jerry Ivey walked out of the back door of the Salina Police Department (SPD) and conversed with his friend and fellow officer, Officer Ron Styles. Ron was coming off of the night shift and had begun handing the car keys for unit 903 to Jerry. Jerry told Ron he had been assigned to 901 for the shift and would be driving unit 901 for the day. This was the last time Officer Ron Styles would ever see his friend.

Officer Jerry Ivey knew beat 901 very well by this time in his career. He had been a policeman for nearly five years. He also knew the road block protocols for One Beat and if he needed to check, he would simply pull out the small roadblock book from the door panel of his cruiser and find his roadblock position. 901 is a small beat as far as its geographical footprint is concerned. It encompasses approximately three to four square miles. In comparison to the other beats, one beat is basically half the size of the neighboring beats. An officer can pretty much travel from one location to anywhere else within the beat in four minutes or less. Jerry was on patrol and it was shaping up to be a gorgeous summer Friday. By 7:30 am, the temperature had reached a comfortable 64 degrees. The day's high would reach 95 degrees. It was a beautiful morning and Officer Jerry Ivey believed it would be a great Friday the 13th.

During the coming robbery, Roy Schultz had a goal. Threaten the clerk with mace. Douse them if necessary and get what he could. That had to be what went through his mind with each crime he committed. So far, he had not killed any of his robbery victims. Although his days were actually numbered, Schultz never considered being caught. He thought he was invincible.

It was at this moment in time, everything was about to change for so many people in Salina. At approximately 8:01 am Roy Schultz pulled to the east of the grocery store's main doors, put his stolen Plymouth Valiant in park and walked toward the front doors of Dillon's Sunset. He carried the canister of mace in his left hand and had hidden his pistol under his shirt at the front of his pants. Schultz nervously entered the store, quickly walking to the cashier's area and forced open the door to the office using his shoulder, where he confronted two employees. Cashier Manager, Bob Peterson and Bob's assistant Cashier, Don Istas. Neither had any idea what evil they were about to encounter.

As Schultz entered the restricted area he threatened both men with his can of Mace and pointed his handgun at Peterson's face, demanding all the money. Both Bob Peterson and Don Istas were ordered to show their hands as Schultz had believed a robbery alarm button may be in the room. With the handgun trained on Bob Peterson, Don Istas collected a large amount of cash laying out on the desk, as well as cash from the open safe. While the robbery was occurring, two female employees Penny Phillips and Kim Baughn, witnessed what was happening and began acting very nervous. Seeing this, Schultz ordered the women at gun point into the cashier area to keep them under his control.

After all the money was put into a brown paper bag, Schultz pulled one telephone line from the wall, and fled the store. He was able to steal approximately $3,000 in cash. Schultz ran to his car and fled east bound onto West Crawford Street. It is unknown the exact route Schultz took after fleeing east on Crawford Street. What is somewhat ironic, and very well may have occurred, was if Schultz turned north onto Phillips Street from Crawford, (as he fled,) he would have driven directly by the west side of the Ivey home during his escape.

Roy Schultz had escaped Wichita without being spotted, which was not all that hard. Wichita had many more escape routes and places to hide than in Salina. Out of town or out of state tags were routine in the larger cities. He was just another chameleon hiding in plain sight in Wichita. Salina in comparison is not a large city. It is small enough to be noticed if you do things to make yourself stand out. Small town cops notice things like out of town or out of state tags. They notice cars they do not recognize. That fact alone would lead most to believe Schultz probably arrived in Salina no earlier than June 12th.

The actual robbery took five to seven minutes to complete, from Schultz parking his car until he sped away from the scene east bound on Crawford Street with cash in hand. As Schultz had gotten in his stolen car, one of the employees followed at a distance and was able to get the vehicle description and license. Several telephone calls were soon received at the Salina Police Dispatch Center regarding a robbery.

At around 8:10 am, Sergeant Herb Summers, who was off duty, sat inside Bee Restaurant on North Broadway, having breakfast. Sgt. Summers was also in possession of his police radio and he heard the all-points bulletin (APB) put out by the dispatcher for a tan or white Plymouth two door car. Sgt. Summers sat in his restaurant chair looking out the window onto Broadway and witnessed a tan passenger car speeding north bound. The restaurant was six to eight blocks north of the grocery store. Sgt. Summers fled the restaurant, got into his car and attempted to chase after the suspect, however he quickly lost sight of the vehicle.

It is unknown what exact route Schultz took between leaving Dillon's Sunset traveling east bound on Crawford and Sgt. Summers seeing the possible suspects' vehicle traveling North on Broadway. It is also possible the vehicle Sgt. Summers saw, may not have been Roy Schultz. However, at some point shortly after, in the area of State Street and College and/or College and Iron Streets, Schultz was seen by a citizen as he stopped and attempted to remove the tag from his stolen Plymouth Valiant. It was suspected that Schultz was trying to switch tags at that location, however the car would later be found possessing the stolen license plate from Sedgwick County, Kansas. The information regarding the possible switching of the tag was dispatched to the roadblock officers. It was reported to dispatch the car then fled north bound from the area of College and Iron Streets.

As the robbery calls poured into dispatch, the shift Supervisor (Officer Flick) ordered all officers not responding to the robbery location to establish surveillance in predetermined road block locations within their beats.

Each beat had designated locations to post during a road block situation. These locations allow an officer to view traffic from a vantage point that would allow for basic 360-degree viewing. One of beat 901's roadblock location was on North Ninth Street, near Thomas park, and the north flood dike area. Jerry quickly headed to his road block location to conduct surveillance. He knew he was looking for a white or tan Plymouth Valiant with a known tag number, occupied by one white male suspect. Within minutes of that report, Schultz drove his get-away car north bound on North Ninth Street, heading straight toward Officer Jerry Ivey's road block location. It was only going to be moments before life for so many would change forever.

Roy Schultz had not planned this robbery well at all. Although he found solace in Wichita's busy neighborhoods, he did not use the same tactics in Salina. He could have easily fled into a busy parking lot, even a packed motel lot, or simply snaked through residential neighborhoods until he got back to his motel and hunkered down for the day. However, he did not take that approach.

He also did not know Salina geographically. As Schultz fled from the robbery, north bound on Ninth Street, he was soon spotted by Jerry Ivey. The roadblock (surveillance post) had worked just as planned,

Dillon's Sunset Plaza c1975. Photograph courtesy of the Smoky Hill Museum.

when implemented into policy so many years before. The road block location book had been taught to Jerry Ivey while in training with Marvin Pratt five years before. Jerry Ivey, now a seasoned officer, knew what he was doing. He had nearly five years of experience, had answered many calls, some more stressful than others. He had been assaulted with a firearm and lived to tell about it. These facts alone made many people ask themselves, why did Jerry make this stop by himself? Why did he not conduct a felony stop with a second and third officer? What occurred in the following ninety seconds would change the Ivey family and the Salina Police Department forever?

Imagine losing a trusted partner, a mentor, or a friend in the line of duty—a person who had your back every single day, who shared the same dangers and sacrifices. That is the reality the Salina Police Department faced on June 13, 1975, when Officer Jerry Ivey was shot and killed. The grief that followed was not just profound; it was life-altering. For many officers, Jerry was not just a colleague; he was a brother. His absence left a void that no one could fill, a silence that echoed through the hallways where his laughter used to resonate.

Even now, decades later, his presence lingers. His badge is

displayed in a quiet hallway—a solemn reminder of his courage. His photograph rests on the End of Watch Wall in the lobby, greeting each officer and visitor with a silent testament to the ultimate sacrifice he made. For those who served alongside him, the sight of these memorials brings both solace and pain. They see Jerry in those artifacts, feel him in the weight of their own badges, and carry the enduring burden of his loss. It's not melodramatic; it's the reality of what it means to lose one of your own.

CHAPTER 9

No Man's Land

As Officer Jerry Ivey ran surveillance on his road block location on North Ninth Street, he kept his head on a swivel. Dispatch had broadcast that a tan or light colored two door car had fled the robbery location. The robbery suspect, described as a white male, 40 years old, armed with a handgun had last been seen in the area of Iron and College Streets. Any vehicles moving on the streets were open for investigation if they fit the description given to the patrol beats. As the morning began warming as mid-June days do, Jerry turned to his left and spotted what he had been looking for, Roy Schultz in the tan get-a-way vehicle. Jerry was in the right fishing hole. It was 8:27 am.

When Roy Schultz drove past Officer Ivey's location, Jerry surely received a shot of adrenalin, similar to landing that big fish during the boring moments of fishing. Jerry had not been hiding behind a building or billboard, he had been parked in the open and Schultz knew that he had been found. However, Jerry, as a seasoned officer knew the protocols on handling robbery suspects. He was not going to rush landing this big fish. He was going to keep the line tight and wait for his back up to arrive.

Jerry radioed dispatch, telling Dispatcher Jim Coddington, he had a vehicle matching the suspect's description heading toward the Interstate on North Ninth Street. Captain Jim Huff remembers hearing Jerry's radio traffic and knew Jerry had found their suspect. "You could just tell he had the right guy, it was in his voice" Captain Huff recalled. Jerry began rolling his patrol car away from his road block point to follow and/or pursue the suspect. After hearing the radio traffic from Jerry, Captain Huff began driving toward one beat to assist Jerry Ivey. According to Captain Huff, everyone knew Jerry had the suspect's vehicle simply by the tone of his voice when he keyed up the mic.

Coddington immediately dispatched Officer Jimmy Miller to back up Jerry with the stopping of the suspect. Because Officer Miller had not been placed in a road block location, and had been freely roaming Salina as a "safety officer," he was a long way from Jerry's location on the north end of Salina. Safety officers drove station wagons and were equipped with EMT type equipment to assist on all emergency calls. Unfortunately, Jimmy had actually been closer to the robbery location than Salina's north end when Jerry Ivey radioed that he had the suspect in view. Officer Miller knew he was minutes and not seconds away. Because of this, Officer Miller literally had several miles of street to travel before he could assist Jerry with a felony car stop. Even running code 3 (lights and siren), Jimmy was not going to be much help if things happened quickly.

Officer Miller was Jerrys best friend. They had worked together since 1970 and they were brothers in the sense of the thin blue line. A number of barbecues and beer drinking sessions had occurred at the Ivey house, which Jimmy had attended. Jimmy and Jerry had also had a handgun pointed at them on a warm summer night in 1973. They had a history while at the Salina Police Department (SPD).

In 1991, Jimmy Miller was asked about the event involving the Ivey shooting. Almost instantly, Jimmy became visibly shaken as he thought back on this terrible day. Jimmy began tearing up and his first response was "He was my best friend." Jimmy, now a veteran Detective was very good at his job. To see Jimmy become instantly emotional was hard to witness. A fresh wound had been opened that never healed. Jimmy described exactly what he saw, how he felt and what he did on that day as Jerry lay dying on the ground.

But I told you, I want to tell you a story. First let's cover Officer Jerry Ivey's traffic stop. At approximately 8:27 am on Friday, June 13, 1975 as Roy Earl Schultz fled north bound from the Dillon's robbery scene, he drove on Ninth Street, toward Interstate 70, on the far north end of Salina. As he did, Schultz drove past Jerry's road block position, which was adjacent to Thomas Park on North Ninth Street. Jerry radioed to dispatch that he believed he had the suspect vehicle traveling north on North Ninth Street. As Jerry began following Schultz's get-a-way car, Schultz began formulating his plan to either out run the patrol officer or somehow shoot it out with the officer. Also at this moment in time, Captain Jim Huff, who had been driving to the store to investigate the robbery, heard Jerry's radio traffic. Captain Huff broke off the robbery call and started heading toward Jerry Ivey's location.

Jerry Ivey was a five year police veteran, a seasoned officer with numerous felony arrests under his belt. He was not taking this traffic stop lightly. As years passed by after this event occurred, there have been some people who believed Jerry Ivey may have had "tomb stone courage" and attempted apprehending Schultz without back up. And from a distant view, it may even look that way. However, do not believe that for a second. It's just not the case.

The SPD had set the road block positions throughout Salina in different geographical locations for the purpose of covering as many thoroughfares as possible. This fact alone put Officer Miller, (even running code 3,) a substantial distance away from the north end of Salina. Under perfect circumstances, Jerry would have simply kept his distance and waited for back up to arrive and assist with a felony car stop. However, this would end up being anything but perfect. While Jerry began following Roy Schultz, and Officer Miller and Captain Huff started speeding toward Jerry's location to back him up, Roy Schultz slowed his get-a-way car and suddenly stopped after purposefully turned onto East Diamond Drive. Doing so put Schultz's car in the Triplet auto plaza parking lot. Schultz did this with the intention of confronting and killing the officer. There is no doubt about that. When Jerry turned onto East Diamond Drive to follow Schultz' car—Schultz suddenly stopped his vehicle. This forced Jerry to stop a short distance behind him. Jerry had instantly entered "no man's land." This occurred at 8:31 am.

Jerry had been put into this situation because of Schultz's actions, not his own, and Jerry had been forced to confront Schultz before Jimmy Miller could arrive. Jerry never intended to complete this stop by himself. It just happened, and was completely forced by Schultz' actions.

Once Jerry was in "no man's land," he had to confront Schultz. What happened next would change the course of time for so many people. Some say Jerry was out gunned. Most experts would disagree with that. Most would take a loaded, single shot .22 pistol against an AR-15 if that's all they had, at least you would still be armed. Jerry's was equipped with his assigned armaments, such as his model 15, Smith and Wesson .38 special, six-shot revolver. Unbeknown to him, he was up against a Browning model "high power" 9mm, semi-automatic pistol with either 13 or 14 rounds. Officer Ivey may have been out gunned with regards to ammunition, however, he had enough firepower to complete the task if given the opportunity.

Another factor that played a huge role in this outcome was that ballistic bullet proof kevlar vests were not available for the police in 1975. And yet another factor, which may have even been a bigger issue than not having a bullet proof vest, was the fact that the SPD had switched from a hollow point bullet to a jacketed .38 special bullet the year before. So what occurred when Jerry was forced to prematurely confront his suspect? How did it go down?

Officer Ivey radioed "He's stopping on me," which indicated the sudden stop by Schultz had surprised him and forced his method of how he would respond. Officer Ivey quickly stopped behind the stolen car and opened his patrol car door and began to hold the suspect at bay with verbal commands, while keeping his revolver available and in the down-ready position. There is no way to know for certain, however, Jerry most surely had drawn his revolver as he exited his patrol car. Roy Schultz, who had no reservation of killing a cop, exited his car holding a can of aerosol Mace in one hand and a pistol concealed behind him in the other. Once out of the Valiant, Schultz started running toward Jerry Ivey. If Jerry would have brandished his shotgun toward Schultz immediately, he probably would have won this battle, however he did not have a crystal ball, so it did not happen. Besides, getting the shotgun from a closed case mounted in front of the front seat is not something a person could instantly do.

As Schultz approached to within ten feet of Jerry, he brandished the mace and sprayed Jerry in the face with it. Schultz then raised the Browning pistol and fired directly at Jerry, striking Jerry in the left side of his chest. The bullet entered Jerry's chest just left of center and severed a portion of his heart.

Jerry had been heavily debilitated by the Mace prior to being shot in the chest. Tear gas in the eyes causes an intense burning and short term blindness. Jerry was helpless as far as being able to see and the gun fight became instantly one sided. The first shot from Schultz's pistol would have been fatal by itself. However, Jerry fought back and returned fire toward Schultz. Blinded, Jerry shot toward the sound of Schultz' gun blasts while Schultz stood in front of Jerry, shooting at him. Jerry's first or second fired shot struck Schultz in the right leg. The jacketed bullet impacted Schultz about one to two inches above the knee cap and toward the outside of his right leg. The bullet punctured Schultz's pants and skin, entered into his outer quadriceps muscle and exited his leg and pant leg. Had the bullet been a hallow point rather than a jacketed round nose bullet, it possibly would have done severe damage to Schultz's leg muscle and possibly even his femur bone, ending the assault right there.

Schultz fired more shots at Officer Ivey and both Ivey and Schultz moved in different directions. As the gun battle blazed on between Schultz and Jerry, bullets whizzed by Jerry but bullets number two through eleven, fired by Schultz did not strike Jerry. Jerry continued bleeding internally and his life slipped closer to the end with every heartbeat. The shootout continued as both men continued fired at the other. Eighteen rounds in total left their handguns.

As Jerry remained blinded by the Mace, he emptied all six shots from his revolver. Schultz, as he continued on his murderous shooting tirade, moved to the passenger side of the patrol car and shot through the windows and doors toward Jerry's position. Each shot missed their mark as several of the bullets struck metal in the front seats, causing the bullets intended for Jerry to veer off and lodge in the interior of the car.

In a panic and mortally wounded, Officer Jerry Ivey, still temporarily blinded, retreated back to the open driver's door of his patrol car to try and retrieve his shotgun. The shotgun was mounted along the front edge of the front seat, sealed in a zipped carrying case. As Jerry attempted to retrieve the shotgun, Schultz ran around to the passenger side of unit 901 and began firing round after round of 9mm ammunition into the car, striking both door windows and striking the rear passenger door numerous times. Schultz, not being an expert marksman was simply trying to shoot Jerry through the car however he could. In Jerry's condition, being blinded and mortally wounded from the chest shot, there was simply no way he was able to reload his revolved by way of either speed loaders or a dump pouch full of bullets. As Jerry struggled to retrieve the shotgun, Roy Schultz, while standing along the passenger side of the patrol car, shot into the passenger window and the last bullet fired struck Jerry in the upper back along his left shoulder blade as Jerry leaned into his patrol car for the shotgun.

This final bullet is believed to have been the fatal round, although either bullet by itself would have been. Jerry had been leaning forward into the car when this last bullet struck. This round traveled downward through Jerry's body and exited his left hip. The bullet slug was later found between his skin and the elastic underwear waist band during the autopsy. The bullet had severed Jerry Ivey's heart as well as his left lung.

A later autopsy showed Officer Jerry Ivey had been shot twice. Jerry's heart and left lung could not have been repaired, even if he had been on an operating table in that parking lot.

After shooting Officer Jerry Ivey, Schultz ran around the rear of the patrol car where Jerry lay dying at the driver's door. Schultz grabbed the shotgun, which had been partially removed from its mount. He then fled with the shotgun to his get-a-way car and sped away after making a U-turn onto Diamond Drive, leaving Officer Jerry Ivey to die in his patrol car.

JIM NORTON

CHAPTER 10

A View From A Witness

The morning at the Triplett Travel Plaza was as normal as any other at about 8:30 AM, on Friday, June 13th, 1975. Over the next four minutes nothing would ever be normal again. Twenty-One-year-old Joe Hay Jr. and his boss, Dave Maxwell were inside the travel store as a tan Plymouth Valiant, being followed by a patrol car began pulling into the parking lot to the southwest of the gas station. As the Valiant quickly stopped, the patrol car did the same. Joe, who had been standing in the doorway, began walking west into the parking lot to see what he could see. Joe stated it did not appear to be a routine or standard vehicle stop to him— something about it felt different.

Joe walked into the parking lot toward a pay phone booth, which stood along the west edge of the parking lot. Joe later stated while thinking about that moment in time, "there is nothing about the car stop that seemed normal to me."

As Joe stood looking at the "car stop," watching what was going on, he saw Officer Jerry Ivey open his car door. Joe knew Jerry personally as Jerry would often stop into the Triplett station for coffee. Joe saw the driver of the Valiant quickly exit and begin running straight at Officer Ivey's location. Soon after, Joe saw a burst of some kind of spray came from the hand of the Valiant driver (Roy Earl Schultz) and Joe could see Officer Ivey was instantly disabled. Joe would describe what he witnessed as something happening "as if time was standing still."

As Joe's mind was processing what he had just witnessed, the first gunshot burst out and Officer Ivey fell backward. Joe Hay ducked behind the phone booth as gunfire bursts seemed to surround him. "It sounded like it was coming from all directions around Officer Ivey and the driver of the Valiant. **Pop,** *pop, pop, pop, pop,* it just went on for what seemed like forever," Joe would later tell investigators. As the gun fire slowed, Joe looked up from his hiding spot and witnessed Schultz shoot through the passenger side of Officer Ivey's patrol car and he saw Jerry fall backward to the ground. Joe saw Schultz run around the back side of the patrol car and to the driver's door where he stood over Jerry Ivey, before grabbing the shotgun from the driver's seat area. Joe watched in terror as Schultz ran while holding the shotgun toward the Valiant, to flee. Joe later told investigators "I didn't think the shooting would ever end, it just went on forever."

Joe Hay Jr. ran toward Officer Ivey before Roy Schultz had even fully committed the U-turn onto East Diamond Drive, to flee. Joe said he was too busy trying to help Officer Ivey to see where the Valiant had sped off to. "It was so unreal; I couldn't believe what I had just seen."

As Jerry Ivey lay on the concrete parking lot of the Triplett Travel Center, Joe Hay tore open Jerry's uniform shirt to stop any bleeding and to check for a pulse. Joe found a bullet wound in the chest area, but found no pulse.

Joe Hay, in a panicked state, held Jerry's head. As he did, Joe saw the police radio mic laying on the driver's seat. "I need help, officer down, he's been shot, help, send an ambulance." Joe screamed over

IVEY BADGE 44

Jerry Ivey's police radio.

As soon as the world heard that transmission, Dispatcher Coddington began sending an ambulance and all available personnel to the shooting scene. Soon after, Joe Hay again keyed up the radio and screamed "officer down, I need a fucking ambulance now, please hurry, he's dying." It was then Dispatcher Coddington ordered the airway cleared for emergency traffic.

A total of eighteen (18) bullets had been fired in this gun battle. Six by Officer Ivey and twelve by Roy Schultz. The passenger side of Jerry's patrol car was riddled with at least seven bullet holes and both windows had been shot out. What seemed like a lifetime of shooting to Joe Hay Jr., in essence took only about thirty to sixty seconds. That one minute of time would change everything for so many people.

As Joe Hay sat on the concrete parking lot holding Jerry Ivey's head, he knew Jerry was gone. Joe felt no pulse, nor did he get any response from Jerry. Joe had never felt so alone. He had just witnessed a tragic murder that would stay with him his entire life. In what seemed like hours to Joe, but was mere minutes, Officer Miller arrived, followed by an ambulance. Jerry Ivey was rushed from the scene by the ambulance while Jimmy Miller stayed to guarded the crime scene.

BULLET HOLES

Bullet holes were found in siding and shattered windows of a storage building along the east portion of the Triplett property. The bullet impacts are likely from Officer Jerry Ivey's revolver due to the direction Jerry fired his first three shots at Schultz. It is unknown which of the six rounds fired by Jerry actually struck Schultz in his right leg, however it was the investigators opinion the first or second shot fired by Jerry would have been the most accurate shot he had taken.

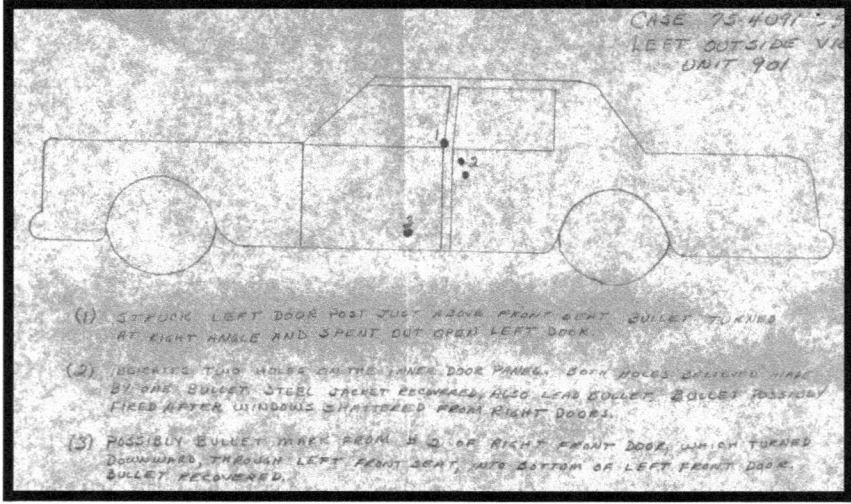

Driver's side damage on unit 901. Diagram by unknown officer.

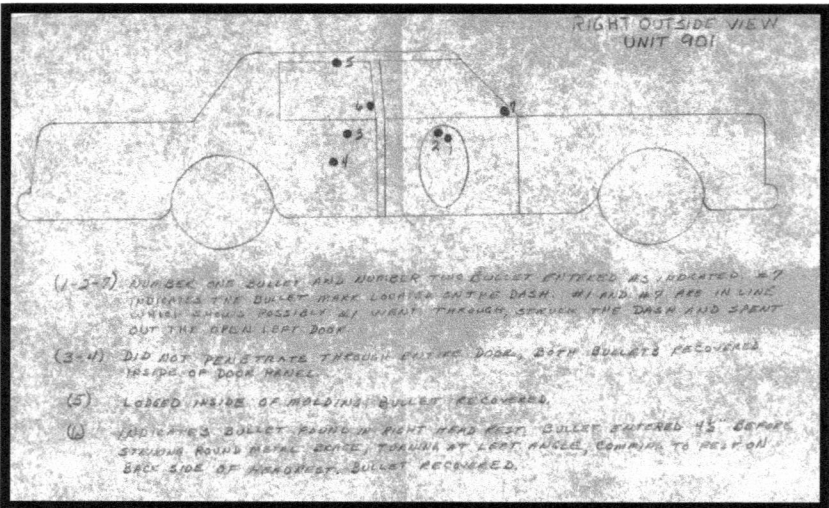

Passenger side damage of unit 901. Diagram by unknown officer.

CHAPTER 11

The Arrest

Schultz had obviously not studied Salina and had little to no knowledge of the geographical area. He could have fled either east or west on Interstate 70 or he could have left town north bound on Old 81 Highway. He chose none of those paths. Instead he fled south bound on Ninth Street, in the direction of Officer Jimmy Miller, Captain Jim Huff and soon, many other officers, straight back into town.

Why had Schultz done this? Probably because it was the path he knew, which would get him back to his motel room. As to why he shot Officer Jerry Ivey, only he could answer that. Soon he would, when asked.

After the murder, Roy Schultz, seeing Officer Miller's lights and hearing the siren, drove into the north driveway of Thomas Park, just east of North Ninth Street. Although the park might have afforded Schultz a brief reprieve away from Officer Miller, it did nothing to shelter him from the many other police cars rushing to the north end of Salina. As Officer Miller arrived on Diamond Drive, he radioed that the suspect was driving south on North Ninth Street away from the scene. Jimmy had chosen to go to Jerry's location. He could see Captain Huff's vehicle a short distance behind him and knew others would soon handle what needed handled. As Officer Miller arrived he quickly realized his friend had died. Overwhelmed by emotions, never having to deal with such a tragedy, Officer Miller started crying. A mixture of complete sadness and furry engulfed him. He sat with Jerry, sobbing as the ambulance, patrol supervisor and back up arrived and took over the scene.

The truth is, Jimmy did everything he could have done. He had not slacked. He had not hesitated. He had done his best to get to Jerry and help. However, it would take years before Jimmy would come to that realization. Jimmy was haunted by his friend's death. It was a trauma that needed counseling, which he never received. Jimmy would take that trauma to his grave when he passed away years later.

As Schultz attempted to get away from the confines of Thomas Park, he drove out of the south entrance and directly into a string of on-coming police cars responding to Officer Ivey's shooting.

To flee that situation, Schultz turned west onto Euclid Street, without realizing it was a dead end road. As he turned right onto Euclid Street, he was confronted by Captain Huff, who had driven his own vehicle from his house, after getting the telephone call of the Dillon's robbery. Captain Huff was going to catch the Monster.

During the research portion this story, Jim Huff was contacted and asked if we could speak about the events surrounding the death of Jerry Ivey. Jim stated; "as long as I live and as bad as my memory may get, there are two things in my life that are so ingrained in me, I could never forget them. One was the day I was married and the other was the day Jerry Ivey died." Jim was willing to tell everything he knew about June 13, 1975. Jim explained how this terrible day all went down. He was willing to divulge the details of the Ivey investigation, to which, he stated he could recite as if it were yesterday.

IVEY BADGE 44

Huff was the Detective Captain and was preparing to leave his home on that Friday morning to start his day when the phone rang. He would typically have driven to the police station; however, dispatch had informed him of the robbery at Dillon's Sunset Plaza. Jim left his home and began driving toward Dillon's when the radio crackled and Officer Jerry Ivey transmitted that he had the suspect's vehicle traveling north on North Ninth Street and would follow the car until back up could arrive.

Moments later, he heard Officer Ivey transmit "The suspect's stopping on me." Seconds after that, Officer Ivey keyed up his mic and stated "he's getting out, I'm going to have to confront him." Jimmy said that was the last radio traffic transmission Officer Ivey ever made and he described feeling "an eerie silence, which seemed to hang over the transmission."

Captain Huff made the decision to forgo the robbery location and head to Officer Ivey's location. He knew another officer would be on scene at Dillon's to start the robbery investigation and get details needed for him to follow up on.

Jim believed sixty to seventy seconds passed before he and all of Salina heard the civilian voice, which we now know was Joe Hay Jr., keying up the police radio and screaming that the officer had been shot, and for everyone to hurry because the officer was dying.

Jim Huff, who had been given the suspect vehicle description raced toward the location where Officer Ivey had been shot. As he did, he witnessed Roy Schultz turn onto West Euclid Street in an attempt to get away. Jim described the following in vivid detail:

> *I followed Schultz' tan Plymouth Valiant at a safe distance until the Valiant had no road left to drive. Euclid is a dead end and abuts into the river flood control dike, west of the city limits. Schultz stopped his vehicle and just sat in the driver's seat facing south west. He was trapped. I knew I had his ass. He had nowhere to go. I stopped a safe distance east of Schultz's car. It was as if my vehicle was somewhat below Schultz's, due to the geography of the location.*

Captain Huff armed with a 30-30 rifle, opened his driver's door and leveled the rifle directly at Schultz's head. He yelled at Schultz "come out of the car, unarmed, place your hands on his head and kneel beside the car." Schultz did not immediately respond. Jim then yelled to Schultz, "son of a bitch, come out unarmed or I'll kill you where you sit."

Captain Huff said Schultz looked at him, saw he was in the sights of a rifle and slowly opened the door, raising his hands above his head. Turning to his right, Schultz faced the suspect vehicle and knelt down with his hands up and surrendered.

Jim tactfully approached Roy Schultz, keeping his rifle pointed at Schultz. As Jim approached to within feet of Schultz, he put his rifle on the ground and quickly placed handcuffs on him, taking him into custody. As the arrest was occurring, off-duty Sergeant Herb Summers, along with Sergeant Bob Clark arrived and Sergeant Clark assisted Jim Huff with walking Schultz to Huff's vehicle.

As Jim and Sergeant Bob Clark were walking Schultz to his (Huff's) car, Captain Ken Brown arrived. Jim Huff stated Captain Brown appeared overly charged with emotions and reached or lunged at Schultz in an attempt to grab him, only to be stopped by Jim who stated, "Capt. I got him. He is under arrest." Schultz then began complaining that he had been shot by the officer and needed medical attention. Jim Huff knew he needed to get Schultz away from the arrest scene as fast as he could, simply because of how emotionally

Flood Control Dike, Salina, Kansas. Arrow indicates murder suspect, Roy Schultz, was led to a waiting police car after he was caught on West Euclid Street. Photograph appeared in the Salina Journal, June 13, 1975.

charged everyone was. By this time, eight or ten officers had arrived at the end of the road where Schultz had been arrested. Schultz was escorted to Jim Huff's waiting car and placed in the back seat.

Once in Huff's car, Jim ordered Sergeant Summers, to get into the back seat with Schultz. Jim admitted the following, saying he "wasn't proud of what I said, however, I told Sergeant Summers take out your revolver, put it against this assholes temple and if he tries anything, blow his brains out." Jim admitted he wished he had not said those words, but he was also somewhat charged and anger was starting to set in. Jim Huff then drove himself, Sergeant Summers and Roy Schultz to St. John's Hospital to get Schultz medical attention for the gunshot he had received during the shootout with Jerry Ivey. Not a word was said on the ride to St. John's. Roy Schultz had been captured.

While at St. John's Hospital, Jim Huff informed the emergency room physician that Schultz had been shot in the leg by a .38 special bullet. It was then the doctor asked Schultz if he had "shot the officer." Schultz acknowledged he had, and when asked why, Schultz replied, "I had to get away."

JIM NORTON

Jail Calendar, 1975. Listing the booking of Roy Earl Schultz. Records, Smoky Valley Genealogical Society.

| Schultz, Roy EARL | Rt 32 Pecos, Texas | 10AM 6-14-75 | 4AM 9-25-75 | Agg Murder - Robbery | HOLD |

Jim Huff was amazed at Schultz' lackadaisical attitude toward killing Jerry Ivey. During an interview after being released from St. John's Hospital, Roy Schultz asked Jim Huff "did the officer die." When told that Officer Ivey had in fact died, Schultz showed no emotions and simply replied "OK."

The arrest affidavit written by Captain Bob Mermis stated the same basic details as provided by Jim Huff. The affidavit names other police officers who assisted at the robbery and arrest scenes. The affidavit depicts the manner in which Schultz committed the robbery at Dillon's Sunset Plaza. In the affidavit, Captain Mermis writes "At the scene of the robbery I met and interviewed Don J. Istas, Kim Baughn and Penny J. Phillips who are Dillon's employees, who witnessed the robbery. They provided Smith (Officer Dave Smith) with the following information. At approximately 8:00 am, 6-13-1975, the suspect entered the store and proceeded to look at a magazine rack. Miss Baughn observed him and recalled seeing him in the store on 6-12-1975, at which time he had been acting in a suspicious manner. Miss Baughn called Miss Phillips to her register and informed her of the suspicious nature of the suspect and asked her "to keep an eye on him."

Mermis' affidavit continues, stating "The suspect was described as being a W/M, 40 to 45 years old, 5'10" to 5'11', approx. 180lbs., with dark collar-length hair. According to the witnesses, he entered the safe area where Mr. Istas was counting money. He produced a blue or black automatic weapon and demanded all the money. He produced a paper bag and proceeded to rob the safe and cash drawers of an estimated $3,000.00 in coin and paper money. After tearing out one of the telephone receivers, he left the store walking toward the east. After he had left the store, Mr. Istas telephones the police department and reported the robbery."

IVEY BADGE 44

"At approximately 8:30 am, 6/13/1975, Officer Jerry Ivey observed a vehicle fitting the description of the suspect's vehicle, which had been broadcast on the police radio earlier by Officer Dave Smith. Officer Ivey radioed the police department that he was stopping a light brown 1964 Plymouth Valiant, 2-door sedan bearing 1976 S/G C 11424 in the area of I-70 and US-81. A few moments later, the police department was notified by a citizen that a police officer had been shot and was down on the pavement at the Triplett Standard Service Station located at US-81 and I-70. Arriving Officers discovered the Officer shot was Jerry Ivey."

Captain Bob Mermis was the Patrol Captain and the commander of the Patrol Division. Although Captain Mermis authored the affidavit, I believe the bulk of the information was given to him by Officer Dave Smith as well as Captain Jim Huff, who had been on both crime scenes.

Although an accurate representation of the events, it is believed Captain Mermis omitted the radio transmission described by Captain Jim Huff, in which Jerry told dispatch moments before his death that "he's stopping on me", which is different than Captain Mermis' account that Jerry radioed he "was stopping the car."

The difference being, that in no uncertain terms did Jerry Ivey stop Schultz' car as a traffic stop. Schultz forced the stop, which forced Jerry in a very dangerous and unforeseen situation.

At the same time Schultz was taken to St. John's hospital for treatment, the police department was working three different crime scenes and Jerry Ivey was transported to Asbury Hospital on Santa Fe. It was there, the emergency room doctor pronounced the official time of death of Officer Jerry R. Ivey, Badge #44.

JIM NORTON

CHAPTER 12

An Unfair Aftermath

As the three crimes scenes were being investigated, those being the Dillon's robbery location, the shooting location of Jerry Ivey and the arrest location of Roy Schultz, Maryann Ivey had loaded her three little boys into her car and began driving to the Dillon's Sunset grocery store, completely oblivious to what had just happened in her world. As Maryann turned the family car from West Crawford into the parking lot at Dillon's, she was blindsided with police activity and patrol vehicles. They basically blocked much of the front of the store. Maryann unloaded the boys and began walking them toward the front doors. However, before being able to begin shopping, she asked someone what was going on. It was at that point in time that the most unfair thing that could ever happen to a loved one, happened to Maryann Ivey.

While standing near the front doors of the grocery store, Maryann was told that the grocery store had been rob and that after the robbery, a police officer had been shot.

Maryann's next question would mar her for the rest of her life. Maryann asked who the officer was that was shot. Someone in the store told her they were not exactly sure, but believed it was possibly Officer Ivey who had been shot. The person who relayed that information to Maryann, had no idea who she was or who her husband was. Maryann's heart sank and she began freaking out. She raced from the store with her three boys in her arms.

In a mad panic, with despair looming over her thoughts, she drove to her mother's home on Morningside Drive and dropped off the boys. She then sped to the police station to learn what she could. Silently, Maryann prayed the entire trip from the Burgess home to the police station, however, as she arrived at the police station things would soon change in her life. Maryann was brought into Chief Woody's office and he confirmed that it had been Jerry who stopped the robber and he had been shot. Neither Chief Woody, nor Maryann was aware that Jerry had been pronounced deceased by the ER doctor minutes before.

Chief Woody and Maryann drove to the Asbury emergency room entrance, where they rushed inside. The scene was chaotic with medical personnel and law enforcement officers gathering around the exam room where Jerry lay on a bed. Despair could be seen on everyone's face. Jerry had died prior to being transported to the hospital. There was simply nothing anyone could do to save him.

Maryann, sobbing uncontrollably, was absolutely as crushed as a person could be. Her world had just fractured. The immense pain and sorrow she felt during those minutes and following hours is unimaginable. She broke down sobbing so uncontrollably that she had to be helped into a separate room. Once inside, the doctor gave her a mild sedative to help calm her.

As saddened and shocked as the Salina Police Department was, Maryann felt that sadness and shock a hundred times more heavily. Maryann Ivey, happy and living her life thirty minutes before, just become a widow, and three little boys became fatherless. It was unimaginable. The pain and sorrow she felt was more than she could handle. She had lost the love of her life and her world was absolutely fractured. There are no other words that can be said about the situation.

As word spread around town, everyone who knew Jerry or Maryann were shocked and terribly saddened. Salina as a whole felt as if it had been violated. One of their proud Police Officer's had been murdered.

Less than an hour later, Maryann's sister, Linda, who was home with her newborn baby, needed to speak with her father about a family matter. Linda, unaware of what had happened to Jerry, called her dad who was working at Burgess Schwinn Cyclery. As Linda called, she hoped her dad would answer the call. Instead, another employee answered and told Linda her dad was unavailable. The employee informed Linda that Jerry Ivey had been shot. No other information was given to Linda. Linda's first thought was Jerry had probably been shot in the arm and everything would be okay, she would call Maryann in a little while. If only that were the case. Linda would soon learn from her father that Jerry had in fact died. She was crushed. Linda would then have to break the terrible news to her husband, Bruce, who was as close to Jerry as anyone in the family.

Linda described her sister, Maryann as the strongest person she knew. Linda was amazed that over the next few months Maryann would show little outward emotions in public. Maryann's sister often wondered just how Maryann must of mourned and suffered with her loss while in the privacy of her own home. The thought broke Linda's heart to imagine it. "She was the strongest person I've ever known," said Linda. She simply could not imagine what her sister was going through.

JIM NORTON

CHAPTER 13

The Outpouring of Grief

After news had broken of the murder of Officer Jerry Ivey and proper notifications were made, a prominent businessman, Charlie Walker, who was personal friends with Chief Woody, arranged for several of his pilots to fly from Salina, Kansas to Gastonia, North Carolina, to gather Jerry's family members. Jerry's parents, brothers, sister and other family members were flown from North Carolina to Salina to be with Maryann and to attend the funeral. The family members arrived on Saturday. The Police Department had begun preparing for the funeral, set to occur at 11:00 am, Monday, June 16th.

Assistant Chief of Police Darrell Wilson, who had been on vacation with his wife, Carol in Utah on Friday, June 13th, 1975, had been enjoying some leisure time at a camp ground when a message was given to Darrell from the camp ground attendant. Darrell had been instructed to contact Chief Woody ASAP (as soon as possible) regarding a dire emergency. During that telephone call, an upset and saddened Chief John Woody told Darrell to cancel all plans and fly home from Salt Lake City, Utah, into Wichita. Darrell was told pilots would pick he and Carol up in Wichita and fly them home to Salina.

Darrell and Carol left their pickup truck and camping trailer at the Utah camp site and flew to Wichita. They were picked up by Charlie Walker's pilots upon landing in Salina. After Carol was driven home, Darrell was driven to the police department for a briefing about the murder and upcoming funeral of Jerry Ivey. Needless to say, both Darrell and Carol were crushed over the news of Jerry's death. Darrell knew it would be on his shoulders, as Assistant Chief to keep the Department together.

On Saturday, members of the Salina Police Department, Saline County Sheriff's Department, and the Kansas Highway Patrol Honor Guards took shifts standing in vigil over Jerry's casket as it was displayed at Ryan's Mortuary. Also, on Saturday morning, June 14th, 1975, a contingency of local Salina Officers and County Deputies wheeled Roy Schultz, who sat handcuffed in a wheel chair into Magistrate Court #308. Schultz was shielded by at least five police officers, as numerous others stood guard at each door or entry point into the court room. Attorney William Mize, anticipating the appointment to become Schultz' Defense Attorney, stood behind the line of officers shielding Schultz.

Judge Gene Penland asked Schultz if he was in fact Roy Earl Schultz. He identified himself as Roy Schultz. Judge Penland then read the two charges to Schultz: First Degree Murder and Aggravated Robbery. At this point, Roy Schultz responded to Judge Penland that $500 of the money he had been in his possession was actually his and he wanted it back. This was the level of empathy or remorse Schultz had shown to the court. County Attorney Jim Sweet told the court they believed all funds in Schultz' possession were stolen and they would remain in evidence. Judge Penland ruled the money would stay in evidence and found Schultz as being indigent. He then appointed William Mize to represent Schultz on all criminal counts. A preliminary hearing was scheduled for June 24th, 1975. After the unusual Saturday morning court proceedings, Schultz was transported back to the Salina Police Department building, where he was being housed in a small holding cell.

On Monday Morning, June 16, 1975, Sheriff's Deputies along with several Kansas Highway Patrol Troopers patrolled the streets of Salina. They did this so local Salina officers could attend the funeral of their fallen officer. Officer Ron Styles pinned the Salina Police Department badge onto Jerry Ivey's uniform shirt as Jerry laid in state, prior to the funeral. City Manager Norris Olson issued an administrative order requiring all flags on city property to be lowered to half-mast to honor Jerry. All business owners and citizens were encouraged to do the same.

Officer Jerry Ivey funeral was attended by hundreds and hundreds of citizens. It was held at the Sacred Heart Cathedral. The funeral was attended by so many friends, family and respectful citizens that people in attendance who could not fit into the church stood as far away as the parking area, outside. There was simply no room left in the church for anyone to sit or even stand.

After the funeral, a Salina Police Department funeral procession led Jerry's hearse to his final resting place at Mount Cavalry cemetery. Every road in the cemetery was packed with numerous agencies police cars, as well as cars of the attendees who found parking within the cemetery. Other mourner's vehicles stretched as far west on Iron Street as the eye could see. Every intersection along West and East Iron Street was blocked by a uniformed officer, stopping all traffic and clearing the way for Jerry's final ride. Hundreds of law enforcement officer's from all over the State of Kansas attended the funeral in full dress uniforms to represent their agencies and bid farewell to a fallen Officer.
Months later, after the funeral and the shock had somewhat diminished, Maryann Ivey met with Stephen Ryan at the Ryan

Mortuary. Maryann was shown how to complete the necessary paperwork to get Jerry a military headstone. The stone Maryann chose was a twenty-four inch by twelve inch, flat granite stone, which was engraved with his personal information and the military rank and service he had been involved in. The US Army would later ship the completed stone to Ryan's Mortuary and the stone was mounted at the head of Jerry's gravesite where it sits today.

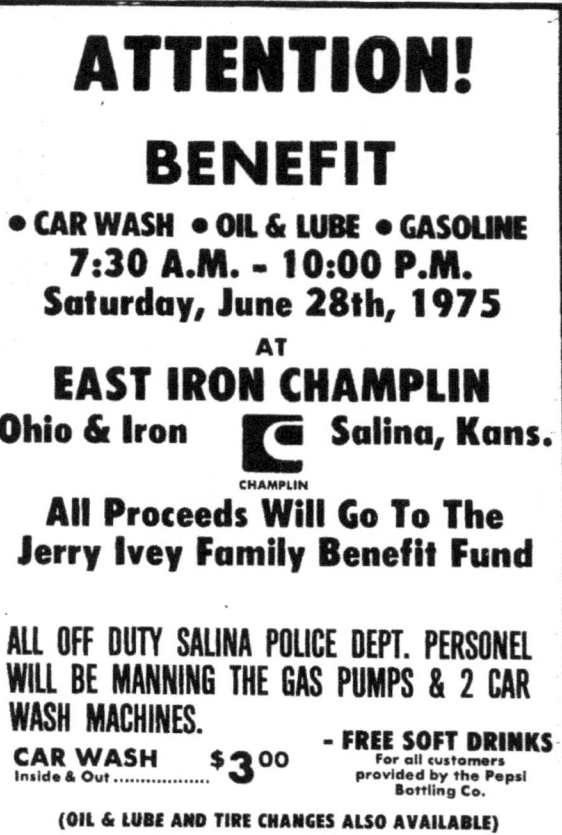

Within days of Jerry's death, the public began showing their generosity toward Maryann and her children, as several memorial funds were put into place. This was 1975, unlike today when someone can go to a computer and open a "Go-Fund-Me" account. Starting a memorial fund was not as easy in that era. By Saturday, the day after the murder, local and state law enforcement members had donated almost $2,000 to Maryann to help with the funeral expenses.

The Salina speedway held a race on Saturday night, June 14th, 1975, and during the race, the race car driver's stopped racing and each walked into the stands with their helmets off and started a collection for the family. By the end of the night, another $723 had been placed in the driver's helmets. A private citizen named Ruth Gordon hand

IVEY BADGE 44

On Saturday, June 28, Salina police officers took over gas pumps and car washes at the East Iron Avenue Champlin Service Station to support Jerry Ivey. They pumped over 4,000 gallons of gas and washed hundreds of cars. Police cadet Daniel Fillmore reported that about three-quarters of the Salina Police Department participated in the event. Photograph courtesy of the Smoky Hill Museum Salina Journal negative collection.

delivered a glass jar with six dollars in nickels and four one-dollar bills to the Police Station. Mrs. Gordon stated she had been saving her nickels for a while and believed the Ivey children needed them more than she did.

On that same Saturday, a jail inmate asked to speak with Sheriff Ervin Hindman. After being allowed to chat with the Sheriff, he told Sheriff Hindman he had read the *Salina Journal* article about Officer Ivey being killed by a robber. The inmate stated he did not know Officer Ivey, however he had two small children at home and if what happened to Officer Ivey had happened to him, he hoped people would assist his wife financially. The inmate asked the Sheriff to remove any money from his commissary funds as he wished to donated the money to Maryann. His donation totaled only five dollars, but the generosity could not be overlooked. It showed the true essence of Salina.

A car wash was arranged by a Girl Scout Troop and all proceeds from the car wash were given to Maryann. The Salina Jaycees, a civic organization, pooled some money together and the group painted the Ivey home at no cost to Maryann. On July 19, 1975, a benefit dance was held at the Salina Labor Building and the entry fees totaled $240. The money was also donated to Maryann. By mid-July, more than $27,000 had been raised and given to Maryann to assist her with her finances.

Printed in the July 22, 1975, *Salina Journal* was an article titled "A poor substitute." The following article tells about several of the donations and how the community came together to help Maryann with future expenses.

> *All the money on earth still would be a poor substitute for a husband and father. But in our material society, it's the only means we have to express our gratitude for men like Jerry Ivey, who died in service of Salina, and our support of those he left behind.*

It could not have been said any better. After all donations were collected for Maryann, the community had donated nearly $40,000. Most of the donations had been received through a fund raising drive headed by the staff at the *Salina Journal*.

CHAPTER 14

The Trial For Roy Schultz

In 1975, the Saline County Attorney's Office was headed by prominent Attorney James Sweet. Known as "Jim" to most who knew him. Jim Sweet had been an assistant County Attorney for the previous eight years and in November, 1974, had won the election to become the Saline County Attorney. A man short in stature with blonde curly hair. Jim was somewhat quiet and unassuming, yet a lion in the court room. Well respected is a very good description of the man who would prosecute Roy Schultz. Schultz's Defense Attorney was going to have his hands full for sure.

As an experienced attorney, Jim would not appear as a "deer in the headlights" while prosecuting a murder suspect. Especially one whose case was truly as open and shut as the Schultz case would be.

On June 14, 1975, Captain Bob Mermis submitted a two-page arrest affidavit to Jim Sweet's office. Jim and his prosecutors began the ball rolling to prosecute Roy Earl Schultz to the fullest extent possible. Although the death penalty had been stricken after 1965, Jim was going to try and get whatever the most severe sentence he could for Roy Schultz.

After Schultz' arrest, medical treatment at St. John's Hospital and an interview with Detectives, he was placed into the Salina Police Department (SPD) jail. This jail was designed to serve as a holding location for short term prisoners. The jail was not adequate for long term housing, nor was it intended for that. Schultz would spend over two months in this jail. The holding jail did not even have full time guards. It was checked on every half hour when occupied. This was a duty performed by the desk sergeant. Normally no felons would have been housed in the SPD jail. It was not set up for long term holding and was never meant for a full time hardened murderer like Roy Schultz. However, Chief Woody let it be known that Schultz was the responsibility of the Salina Police Department. There would not be a transfer to Saline County. Woody was heard saying, "This bastard belongs to us."

The SPD jail, if you wanted to call it that, consisted of six cells. Three cells along the east half and three cells across the hallway on the west half. The east cell doors faced inward into the hallway and the west cells did the same. The hallway dividing the two halves was simply a way for an officer to walk the perpetrator into their awaiting cell. The jail was simply a large square room, with outer walls make of cinder block and the inner walls made of one and a quarter inch round steel bars. The cells did not have beds. Just a raised concrete area, where a flimsy jail mattress could be thrown onto the floor. Absolutely zero privacy was given to anyone in the cells, who was unfortunate enough to find themselves locked within.

Public Defender William D. Mize, was an intelligent and capable lawyer, however he had been handed a very emotionally charged case that through all viewpoints, appeared to be as "Slam Dunk" as criminal cases go. He knew the cards were stacked against him.

Most defense attorneys, especially most public defenders, really do not expect to get their clients off of serious criminal charges, they simply want to make sure the system is fair and their clients get treated impartially. Attorney Mize knew what he was up against and only had one avenue to pursue for the defense for Roy Schultz. That was an insanity defense.

As in many prosecutions, especially one of this magnitude, motions were going to be filed, primarily by Mr. Mize on behalf of Schultz, and filed they were.

One of the first motions filed by Attorney Mize was a motion asking the court to order the removal of Schultz from his current jail location at the SPD facility and to move him to the Salina County Jail, ran by Sheriff Ervin Hindman. This motion would give him much easier access to Schultz and stop Chief Woody and his officers from having access to Schultz.

In the motion, Mr. Mize states the following:
1. The Defendant has been subjected to and continues to be subjected to both physical and mental distress and abuse.

2. That the Defendant has suffered and continues to suffer demeaning and degrading treatment.

3. That the Defendant has been deprived and continues to be deprived of commonly accepted and customary privileges (*sic*) permitted all inmates of the Saline County jail. And as a result of said unequal, cruel and unusual treatment, has been denied his constitutional rights as guaranteed under the 8th and 14th amendments of the Constitution of the United States and the Constitution of the State of Kansas.

This motion was heard by Judge Haggard. It was a valid motion made by Attorney Mize. It is not a misstatement to say Schultz was not treated well by anyone on the SPD or anyone within their building. From accounts of people present inside the Salina Police Department in 1975, it would be fair to say that during his incarceration, Roy Schultz had not been treated with "kid gloves" by anyone at the police department. The motion was rightfully granted and Schultz would be moved into Sheriff Hindman's custody, after spending two months in the SPD jail cell. This motion was filed in part because Schultz was not allowed to sleep more than thirty minutes at a time. The SPD had an indoor shooting range located directly below the holding cells and target practice seemed to occur much more often after the death of Officer Jerry Ivey. It was also a result of Schultz being given a lack of toilet paper when needed and not being spoken to in the nicest of terms, as a few examples of how things went for Schultz.

The next motion asked for Schultz to be transferred to the Shawnee County Jail for a short period of time, so Schultz could be examined by doctors from Menninger's psychiatric hospital in Topeka. This motion was also granted at Mr. Mize' request. Between July 25 and August 8, 1975, Schultz was interviewed several times by doctors while in Topeka, Kansas. Mr. Mize was playing the only card he had and that was to try and get Schultz diagnosed as insane or otherwise unfit for trial.

Mr. Mize was going to try and prove Schultz was insane under "The McNaughton Rule," which states a person did not know the difference between right and wrong. After the motion was filed, the *Salina Journal* printed in an article stating the rule "is one of the most stringent legal tests of insanity used in this country." That was Mr. Mize' only legal card to play. The writing was on the wall and that card would be played when the time was right.

Needless to say, after all the interviews conducted by doctors at Menninger's Hospital, the tests had failed to determine Schultz was insane. If there is a box to check on the test results page stating the patient was just an asshole, that box should have been checked in this case.

After a long preliminary hearing was presented in front of Judge Haggart, Schultz was bound over on the charges of first degree murder and robbery. After the preliminary hearing, Mr. Mize had an even better idea of what he was up against and how he would proceed. Attorney Mize had one more card in his hand, and he would have to play it next. Jim Sweet and his assistant Dan Boyer had laid out an airtight case and were ready to proceed to trial. Soon a trial date was set.

Attorney Mize' next motion filed, was a motion for a change of venue. Seldom, if ever during a cop's career do they agree with a motion filed by any defense lawyer, however, any officer on the Salina Police Department would undoubtedly have to agree with this motion, as did Judge Haggart. There really was no way this trial could be conducted in Salina in a fair manner. Salina is a close knit community and when a police officer is killed, people talk. Public opinion had been sealed in stone. Schultz was guilty and needed to hang. That was the opinion of most if not all of Salina's citizens.

Through diligent hard work, Attorney Mize was able to identify many people who were willing to sign their names to an affidavit stating they had formed an opinion in the case and who believed a fair and impartial trial was impossible to achieve in Saline County District Court. Attorney Mize and his team found citizens from all walks of life, who resided in Saline County and who stated under oath they had conversations with people regarding the Dillon's robbery and the death of Officer Jerry Ivey. They also swore under oath they felt there was so much prejudice against Roy Earl Schultz, that he could not obtain a fair and impartial trial in Salina County District Court. In all, Attorney Mize had twenty-two signed affidavits from citizens.

The citizens, whom had sworn under oath for Attorney Mize, were employees of law firms, employees of Saline County departments, laborers in the farming community, and even retirees. Attorney Mize had done his homework and was trying his best to not only make Jim Sweet's life harder, but to somehow represent Schultz with an aggressive defense.

During the August 20th, 1975, hearing to get venue changed, Attorney Mize marched witness after witness into court to testify. These witnesses consisted of managers from the *Salina Journal*, KSAL radio, KSKG radio, KINA radio, Salina public TV channel 6 news and others. Attorney Mize questioned them about the amount of public dissemination their platforms had reported regarding the Ivey's death or any other related matters.

Mr. Mize' also called Arlo Robertson, the *Salina Journal's* office manager. Mr. Robertson was in charge of the largest fund collection program put forth for Maryann Ivey. He helped raise money for Maryann Ivey, which had raised a total of over $27,000. Arlo Robertson stated there had been 910 people who had contribute to Maryann Ivey's fund through the Salina Journals collection process.

Attorney Mize had done all the leg work he needed to ensure Judge Haggart would have no choice but to change venue for these proceedings. When this occurs, the court must send out feelers to counties of similar size and population to see where a trial could be moved. The trial must be far enough away from direct publicity, and have a similar population demographic.

Judge Haggart and the Salina County Court Administrator settled on Riley County as being the location for the Schultz trial. Jim Sweet, Dan Boyer and a few assistants in the County Attorney's office were set and ready for trial with many subpoenas for their witnesses having already been served. The Salina Police Department was ready, Jim Sweet was ready, Public Defender William Mize was ready and on the morning of October 7, 1975, a jury in Manhattan, Kansas, had been chosen and seated.

On that morning, at exactly 11:23 am, as the trial was ready to proceed, Attorney Mize announced to the court that Roy Earl Schultz wished to waive his right to a jury trial and Schultz wished to change his plea and was ready to plead Guilty. This came as a shock to County Attorney Jim Sweet and probably irritated Judge Haggard after doing all the work to seat the jury. A full transcript of the interview and exchange between Attorney Mize and Schultz was prepared.

During the interview, Attorney Mize asked Schultz on the record: "Is it your wish at this time to withdraw your former plea of not guilty by reason of insanity and enter a plea of guilty to both charges contained in the information? That is, the Aggravated Robbery and the charge of First Degree Murder?"

To this, Schultz answered, "Yes."

Attorney Mize then asked Schultz if he was changing his plea to guilty under advise from his counsel, to which Schultz replied "I'm doing it of my own free will."

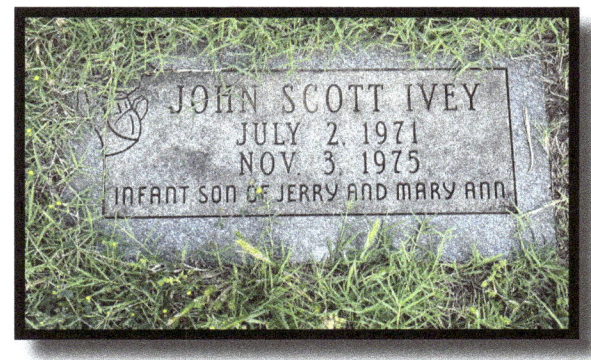

Attorney Mize stated to Roy Schultz, "I'm not advising you to plead guilty."

Schultz then repeated, "I just said, I'm doing it on my own free will."

With that, Judge Haggart dismissed the jury and found Roy Earl Schultz guilty of robbing the Dillon's Sunset grocery store and for the first degree murder of Officer Jerry Ivey.

Roy Schultz was sentenced to a term of Life in Prison along with a consecutive ten-year sentence for the grocery store robbery. Schultz stood at the court podium and showed little emotion to the sentence of life in prison. After court, Schultz was transported back to the Saline County Jail to await transfer to a Kansas State Prison. Afterwards, a newspaper reporter felt the need to ask Maryann Ivey what her feelings were about the guilty plea and the life sentence, to which she replied, "I don't care, just so he gets what he deserves." Maryann was so deep into mourning and carrying the feeling of loss, she was numb to the process.

Before Maryann could even catch her breath from the stress she was under, something else happened.

Exactly twenty-seven days after Schultz pled guilty to killing Jerry Ivey, Maryann would be hit with yet another horrifying loss. On November 3, 1975, four and a half months after losing her husband, her oldest son, John Scott Ivey died of complications from his earlier illness. In less than five months, Maryann Ivey's world was crushed twice. Please let that sink in for a minute.

The sorrow and utter overwhelming sadness that was forced upon this poor wife and mother is unthinkable. Anyone who had any heart was weeping for her. Maryann lay to rest, her son just a few feet to the east of her husband.

During a conversation with retired Lieutenant Ron Styles, Ron was asked about the funeral of little John Scott Ivey. Ron said he and most members of the SPD attended this second funeral. Ron said it was the sentiment of almost all SPD Officers who knew how close Jerry and little Scott were, that little John Scott Ivey had died of a broken heart over the loss of his daddy. Ron remembers all the many times where you could find Jerry running around or even at home off duty, and finding little Scott either at Jerry's side or in his arms. They now lay side by side and are in God's eternal care.

Sheriff Ervin Hindman, Rolled up newspaper featured in the Salina Journal, October 8, 1975.

Years after the passing of little John Scott, Maryann's youngest son, Jerry Ivey II spoke with his mother about the deaths of his dad and brother. Jerry II remembers his mother, Maryann telling him she was so overwhelmed with grief from losing Jerry, she did not have any emotions left in her to even cry for John Scott's death. Maryann had been emotionally wiped clean. The pain was simply too much for her to bare.

On October 5, 1975, as Roy Schultz was escorted from his cell at the Saline County Jail to the waiting prison bus, a jailer with the Sheriff's Department revealed a makeshift club found in Schultz's cell. A photograph published in the *Salina Journal* captured Sheriff Ervin Hindman holding what appeared to be a rolled-up magazine or newspaper, stiffened with an unknown substance. The look of shock on Hindman's face said it all. The people of Salina were eager to see the end of Roy Earl Schultz, a man they viewed as a monster.

CHAPTER 15

The Prison Break
&
The Angry Woody Rant

Within a few weeks of being sentenced to prison, Schultz was taken to Lansing Correctional Facility in Lansing, Kansas. He was assigned Kansas prison number K0007895. Lansing is one of Kansas' largest prisons and is located north west of Kansas City, Kansas.

On July 19, 1977, he and fellow inmate Larry D. Miller "commandeered a work truck" from within the prisons grounds. Schultz and Miller crashed the truck through a gate and through heavy gun fire from the guards, both felons escaped. Schultz crashed the truck five hundred feet from the prison walls and both men ran to freedom. Schultz was loose again.

After exiting the prison, the escapees ran across the street to a service station, where they assaulted a man who was pumping gasoline into his station wagon. The escapees punched the man, knocked him to the ground and fled west in the stolen car.
It would not be an exaggeration to say that Salina Police Chief John Woody was more than livid with the news of the Kansas Department of Corrections allowing Schultz to escape custody. Chief Woody not only wanted the Kansas Department of Corrections' heads to roll, he was terrified Roy Schultz would return to Salina to seek revenge on the public, the prosecutors, his officers and himself. Chief Woody went on a media rampage to let the public know Schultz had escaped and that it was all the fault of the Kansas Department of Corrections.

On July 20, 1977, *Salina Journal* ran an article titled "Angry Woody blasts legislators and Society." It was easy to see where Woody's true feelings fell. As Woody sat in his office, in his swivel chair preparing for an evening face to face news briefing with local newspaper reporters, Woody first set out a grim framework for what was about to take place. "You are talking to a Bitter Man," Woody proclaimed. Everyone in the room could see that Woody was about to lose his temper, and everyone in the room knew why.

"A grim visage showed the intensity of Woody's feelings," wrote one reporter. Woody then began. "I hope some of our legislators who voted against capital punishment will take a good look, because I truly feel before this time tomorrow, Roy Earl Schultz will kill another police officer." In retrospect, Chief Woody was not that far off. However, a newspaper reporter named Don Henry would later print "Twenty-four hours after the breakout, Woody's macabre prophecy has not come true. Schultz and Larry Miller, still at large, were not known to have injured anyone in their flight." This last statement by the reporter would be far from the truth. After the prison break, it had taken Schultz less than ninety seconds to hurt his first victim and less than an hour to hurt two more.

The prison break, reported in several newspapers had occurred when Roy Schultz and another convict named Larry D. Miller had been working together in the prison industrial compound. It happened when a large state truck driven by another state inmate, along with a guard (passenger) backed up to a loading dock.

Warden Oliver stated that as the officer got out of the truck to direct the prisoner (driver) into the unloading dock, the driver was attacked. Schultz and Miller had snuck along the driver's side of the truck and jumped the driver while brandishing knives and secretly-fabricated shivs. The two convicts dragged the driver from the vehicle, throwing him to the ground. The convicts commandeered the truck and began their escape. Warden Oliver stated, "They took the truck and crashed it through two railroad gates and a barricade. An Officer in the tower 50 yards away opened fire on the vehicle and shot the front end five times, but was unable to wound either escapee."

The disabled truck with it's steering and motor crippled, rolled to a stop about 150 yards outside the prison gates near a service station. Immediately after, Schultz and Miller ran to the station and "strong armed a fellow at the gas pumps and took his car."

After stealing the car from the citizen, Schultz drove himself and Miller out of the area and they ended up about fifteen miles away at a home located on the outskirts of Tonganoxie, Kansas. The home happened to belong to newspaper publisher J.M. Nieberger. It was never learned why Schultz had picked the Nieberger home to rob, however after pulling into their country driveway, Schultz and Miller crashed through the front door of the Nieberger's home. Schultz and Miller found Mrs. Nieberger and her three-year-old granddaughter sitting in the living room. Schultz and Miller then tied up Mrs. Nieberger and ordered her to keep the child quiet or they would hurt them both. Mrs. Nieberger, terrified and in shock over the intrusion did as she was told.

Mrs. Nieberger was tied up with twine and after rifling through rooms, cabinets and drawers, the escapees stole a .38 caliber revolver, which had been stored in the Niebergers bed stand, along with some currency and later, the family's Ford Thunderbird. Schultz stole clothing belonging to Mr. Nieberger who was not home. He changed into the clothes, leaving his prison uniform for the cops to use to identify him. Mrs. Nieberger told the convicts that her husband would be notified if she was not able to drop the grandchild off at a certain time. This lie told by Mrs. Nieberger was believable enough to get the convicts to leave shortly thereafter. After the escapees left the Nieberger residence, law enforcement was still unable to locate either of them. The escapees left the stolen vehicle from the service station in the garage of the Nieberger's home when they swapped it for Mr. Nieberger's brand new Thunderbird.

After news of the prison escape, Chief Woody called a special roll call briefing at the SPD, which was attended by uniform patrol and detectives. Chief Woody let it be known he was extremely upset and concerned Schultz would return to Salina to seek revenge. Most of his police officers did not hold those same feeling about Schultz returning. They suspected Schultz would head anywhere except Salina, Kansas. An unofficial verbal "shoot on sight" order had been instructed by Chief Woody, in the event Schultz did return. Within a few hours of giving the order, mini-14 rifles were purchased and placed in every SPD marked patrol car.

Woody went on to lament against the State Legislators who he felt were responsible for this escape. Woody felt the laws were being written to aid convicts instead of the good, god fearing citizens of the State of Kansas, they were elected to represent. Woody was correct with most of his thinking on this matter. Woody was quoted as saying, "Those Legislator's won't be stopping the get-a-way car tonight, but one of my young police officer's might be."

Woody was then quoted saying the best quote of his entire rant, when he spoke about Schultz breaking out of a maximum security prison by smashing through a gate in a truck. Woody openly irritated, proclaimed "I don't know how you can get a truck into a 4 by 8-foot cell, and a 4 by 8-foot cell is what I think of, when I think of a maximum security prison, but because of pressure exerted by certain groups we have to put (Inmates) on a 160-acre farm with running water, or we are being too hard on them." Woody would continue fuming for days. Officers seemed to walk on egg shell while around Chief Woody for the next week. Most simply stayed clear of him and his wrath.

Needless to say, Roy Schultz never returned to Salina. After leaving the Nieberger home, the convicts headed east. East to St. Louis, Missouri, where their crime spree would continue.

It was Friday, July 22, 1977, three days after the escape and kidnapping of Mrs. Nieberger and her granddaughter, when at about 6:00 pm, Schultz and Larry Miller parked their stolen Thunderbird in a mostly empty parking lot. To Schultz, it did not matter if the business was open or not. He would either burglarize it or rob it; this did not really matter to him. He was getting guns if there were any inside. As the convicts walked to the front doors, they found the store open, but empty of customers. Tom McGregor Inc. Sporting Goods Store in south St. Louis had just become target number one. Schultz armed with the stolen .38 revolver from the Nieberger residence, found the store owner and pointed the weapon at his face and ordered him into the center of the business. The owner, Thomas McGregor and his father, Robert as well as Thomas' two sons were then forced into the basement of the building at gunpoint. Once in the basement and clear of anyone's view who might wonder into the store, Miller and Schultz used electrical tape to bind Thomas and Roberts' hands and feet. Schultz did not bind the children, however he threatening them with death if they moved away from the basement wall where they were forced to sit.

Schultz returned upstairs into the main business and raided the store of twenty-two firearms and six knives. Shoving the stolen items into a duffel bag he had taken off the shelf from the camping department area. Schultz and Miler soon left the store after loading the stolen items into the Nieberger's stolen Thunderbird. For good measure, Larry Miller demanded Robert McGregor to empty his pockets and found the car keys to Robert's vehicle, which was parked in the front parking lot. Miller stole the McGregor car while Schultz kept possession of the Nieberger Thunderbird.

As the escaped convicts fled from the sporting goods store, they hid out at an unknown location for several hours. Also, after the robbery was finished and the McGregor's believed they would survive, the oldest McGregor son, who was six years old, cut his dad and grandfather free and all four escaped the building from a basement window along the rear wall of the store. It was nearly 8:00 pm by the time police were notified.

About four hours after the McGregor store robbery, at around 10:00 pm, Schultz and Miller not feeling fulfilled, walked into a grocery store south of St. Louis, Missouri, as it was preparing to close. Both armed suspects forced their way into the business office, where they stole a substantial amount of cash. The convicts had screamed at the clerk to fill a paper bag with the cash and after doing so, the clerk lay on the floor in the fetal position, waiting to be shot to death. The robbery was absolutely terrifying for the clerk. This was also the last location where both Roy Schultz and Larry D. Miller were ever seen together.

Due to sloppy work on Roy Schultz's part, he had forgotten he had laid down the stolen .38 special revolver on a shelf in the McGregor Sports store. Schultz had been so busy filling the duffel bag with guns, he had failed to retrieve the .38 special before he fled. Leaving the revolver for the police to find. It was all the information they would need to identifying their suspects. The gun was not only reported as being stolen from Mr. Nieberger's residence in Tonganoxie, Kansas, it also contained Roy Schultz's finger prints. Within hours, law enforcement all around the Illinois region was on the lookout for Roy Schultz and Larry D. Miller.

The day after the St. Louis crime spree, Schultz turned up on foot at a small car lot in Pekin, Illinois. Schultz left the stolen Thunderbird parked a few blocks away. He had apparently felt he needed to change cars. At the Pekin used car lot, he purchased a car with cash and demanded no paperwork be issued for the transaction. Schultz left the car lot in an older passenger car and the Nieberger's Thunderbird was never seen by the car dealer. It would be several days before the stolen Thunderbird would be found, and the connection between Schultz and the used car dealer was made by the police. As a result, law enforcement wrongly believed Schultz would continue using the Nieberger's stolen car in his plight for freedom. His ***only*** concern was stealing anything he found enticing. With the cops not knowing where Schultz was or what he would be driving, they were in the pursuit of either Schultz or Miller. Little did they know that Schultz's next crime spree would be what nightmares were made of.

Inmate/escapee Larry Miller was re-captured a few days later in Denver, Colorado. He had driven the stolen vehicle taken from the McGregor Sporting Goods robbery. When interviewed by police, Miller told them that Schultz had wanted to kill Mrs. Nieberger while in the Tonganoxie home, however Larry Miller claimed he have talked Schultz out of committing an unnecessary murder. During his interview, Miller told police that Roy Schultz was the "hardest dude" he had ever met. He informed the police that Schultz wanted to kill Mrs. Nieberger because she had lied about her husband's Thunderbird being out of gasoline, in an attempt to persuade him from taking the car. When Schultz returned from the garage after checking the Thunderbird's fuel gauge and finding the car full of fuel, he became so enraged over the lie, he nearly made her pay with her life. Miller claimed he stepped in and calmed Schultz down enough to get them to just leave and keep running. Schultz was wound tight and ready to explode. Explode he soon would.

JIM NORTON

CHAPTER 16

Repeating Failures

Victims' names have been omitted for privacy reasons.

What happened next is almost unbelievable. It was like something out of a horror movie plot. The second most heinous crime Roy Schultz ever committed and thank God the victims survived the ordeal.

On Sunday, July 24th, 1977, seven days after escaping the prison in Lansing, Kansas, Roy Schultz drove his newly purchased car south along an Illinois state highway. He was heading for Peoria, Illinois, however his car broke down outside the city limits of Washington, Illinois. Schultz pulled the car off the roadway and onto the shoulder and waited, deciding what his next move would be. Minutes later, a young husband and his wife along with their two minor children who were as peaceful and friendly as anyone could be, stopped to see if they could help the stranded driver. The wife, who was eight and a half months pregnant with the couple's third child sat in their car as her husband got out and approached the stranded man. The stranded man just so happened to be escaped murder Roy Earl

Schultz. As the husband approached, Schultz produced a handgun and pointed it at his face, ordering the husband back into his car. Schultz would than kidnap the now terrorized family and ordered them to drive him to a Bloomington, Illinois motel. Schultz forced the wife into the center of the front seat and he placed a handgun against her bulging belly, as he sat in the front passenger seat. What occurred in the following six hours is so mind boggling it almost cannot be believed, but happen, it did. During the first half hour of the kidnapping, Schultz ordered the family to drive into Bloomington, Illinois, where Schultz forced them to stop at a liquor store. Schultz forced the husband to purchase beer and Scotch. He threatened to kill the wife and kids if the husband did anything out of line. Shortly after leaving the liquor store, the families car broke down. With few options at his disposal, Schultz summoned a taxi cab to take the family and himself to a Bloomington motel. Schultz continued telling both parents that any resistance by any of the family and he would kill each of them. Just Schultz's presence alone caused extreme terror in both parents. These people were God fearing, law abiding citizens who had never hurt anyone. They just wanted to raise their children and live a happy life.

A few minutes later, while inside of the taxi, the wife silently mouthed "help us, call police" to the cab driver, who smiled and nodded as if he would do so. But he never did. The wife had felt a ray of hope at some point during the taxi ride, and believed the cab driver would help her family. Instead, Schultz, began fumbling with the large bag he held. As he did, he spilled a box of .38 special ammunition onto the floorboard of the cab. As the bullets rolled around on the floorboard, both kidnapped parents felt the taxi driver might stop and possibly run away or summons some type of help. The cab driver did not stop or run away, or do anything to get the police's attention. Instead he pulled over and helped Schultz pick up the bullets from the floor and put them back in the box. Dread weighed down on the kidnapped family as if they were wearing lead vests. Totally terrorized, in complete disbelief of what was happening to them, they continued doing what Schultz ordered.

After the taxi dropped the family and Schultz off at the motel, Schultz forced the husband to pay for a room using the threat of death to his wife and children if he strayed from the plan. And the cab driver never notified the police. Once Schultz and his victims were inside their room, Schultz ordered food from the motel restaurant asking for it to be delivered to the room. It was then that Schultz began drinking heavily and it was then his truly ugly side appeared. After ordering food, Schultz tied up the husband and forced him at gunpoint onto the bedroom floor. Schultz then ordered the wife and their five-year-old daughter to strip naked. Once that was accomplished, Schultz stripped naked as well. Clearly sexual assault was on his mind. About twenty minutes after placing the food order, a young male employee knocked at the door to deliver the food. As Schultz opened the door, the delivery boy looked inside and saw Schultz standing naked with the right side of his body covered by the open door, as well as witnessing the husband bound and laying on the floor. Apparently this did not raise any red flags for him either and he also failed to tell his manager or call the police. The young man did mention what he had seen to another employee, who felt it best for them to stay out of the guest's business and not become involved. No one was coming to help.

Out of respect for the victims, I will not describe in explicit details any of Schultz's sexual actions.

Schultz, however did force the terrorized wife to perform a felony sex act upon him. As Schultz continued drinking, he ordered the husband into the bathroom. The husband was told if he opened the bathroom door his wife and daughter would be shot. After sexually assaulting the wife, Schultz began to sexually assaulting the five-year-old child. The terrorized wife, seeing the viciousness of Schultz's action knew she had to act to stop him and protect her daughter, even if it cost her life. Within seconds of the child being assaulted, the wife's inner Momma Bear came out with a vengeance. As any terrorized victim would, the basic instinct of survival kicked in. She knew she had to fight for her life and the lives of her family. She was a hero mom and she was about to prove it to the world.

While Schultz' attention was on the child, the wife grabbed the Colt .45 semi-automatic handgun from under Schultz' armpit as he lay naked on the bed. She pointed the gun at Schultz's head and pulled the trigger, hoping to blow Schultz's brains against the wall, however nothing happened. The pistol had a loaded magazine, however no bullet had been chambered. She did not know how to function the handgun to load the chamber and the gun had failed to fire. Swinging the gun as hard as she could, she struck Schultz in the head as if holding a hammer. Blood flew from the open flesh wound as Schultz's head bent downward, causing his eyes to close as the wife screamed for her husband to come help her. As he freed himself, he rushed into the main bedroom area not knowing what he might find. What he found was horrifying. Schultz staggered and stood with blood gushing down the side of his face from the head wound caused by several Colt 45 hammer blows. Schultz had been struck numerous times in the head as he staggered around trying to grab his victim. The wife then threw the handgun toward her husband, however the gun landed on the floor beside him. Schultz lunged toward the gun but the husband grabbed it before Schultz could. In a panicked and terrorized state, the husband pointed the gun at Schultz's head and pulled the trigger with the same result. After the handgun failed to fire a second time, both men began a vicious physical fight as punch after punch were thrown by the husband. As Schultz was being battered by the husband, his wife began bashing Schultz over the head with an empty beer bottle. Over and over she smashed his skull, cutting him badly but Schultz continued fighting and seemed invincible. The smell of copper from Schultz's blood splatters filled the room. As she continued striking Schultz in the head, Schultz and her husband continued with their fierce struggle for their lives.

As the fight continued, the wife began kicking Schultz in the legs and ribs with all her might. Each man landed punches from closed fists, however Schultz had been injured badly enough that his blows did not stop the assault against him.

As Schultz became more and more bloody from being struck in the head with the handgun and a beer bottle, the wife found the heaviest item she could and continued the assault on Schultz. She ripped a heavy bedside lamp from the table and began pounding Schultz in the side, ribcage, head and legs with all her might.

The beating of Schultz was so severe it resulted in several skull fractures, broken rib bones and a fractured left shin bone just above his left ankle. The husband and wife had done their best to kill Schultz as they beat him to near unconsciousness. The family had done everything in their power to survive. With the husband exhausted and the wife terrifyingly worn down, Schultz was able to somehow open the motel room door and crawl out of the room and onto the second floor breezeway. There Schultz was met by two police officers, who had been eating at a café in the motel. They had heard the violence occurring in the motel room and went to investigate. As Schultz crawled from the room and then staggered like a naked, bloody zombie who was near death, he was arrested. Schultz as well as the wife and the five-year-old child were transported by ambulances to separate hospitals. This unbelievable ordeal was finally over.

The husband and wife would make out a police report and after all the evidence was collected from the motel room, the police found Schultz had a bag containing a total of five other handguns and almost $6,000 in cash. Shortly after the arrest, law enforcement was able to identify Schultz as being the murderous prison escapee from Kansas, as well as the robbery suspect of the McGregor Sporting Goods store and the grocery store robbery outside of St. Louis, Missouri.

Schultz would be charged with multiple counts of aggravated kidnapping, simple kidnapping, deviant sexual assault and indecent liberties with a child, among other felonies as a result of this final rampage.

The emotional toll this peaceful, loving family had to endure during the kidnapping and attack would not end with Schultz's arrest. That was especially true for the young daughter. Her inner trauma would stay with her for most of her life.

The wife was later interviewed by police and was even quoted in the St. Louis Post Dispatch. While describing the moment she grabbed the gun, she stated "I couldn't believe I had it. He went after me to get it. I tried to fire it but I couldn't….I screamed for my husband and I flung the gun to him." "They both went for it, he tried to fire it and they then began to wrestle." She would continue by saying "I wanted to kill him, I tried too. When we aimed, we aimed for his head. The police and hospital said they wished we would have killed him." She then described how emotionally exhausted she and her husband were.

With regards to all the failures of the citizens to come to their aid during the ordeal, the husband stated, "I had asked the taxi driver to call the police twice, once he said okay and the other time he whispered gotcha, but I guess he never did." Regarding the spilled bullets in the taxi, the wife described the incident stating, "at one point a box of bullets spilled inside the cab. You would think that would have convinced the driver, but what do you think he did, he helped Schultz pick up the bullets?"

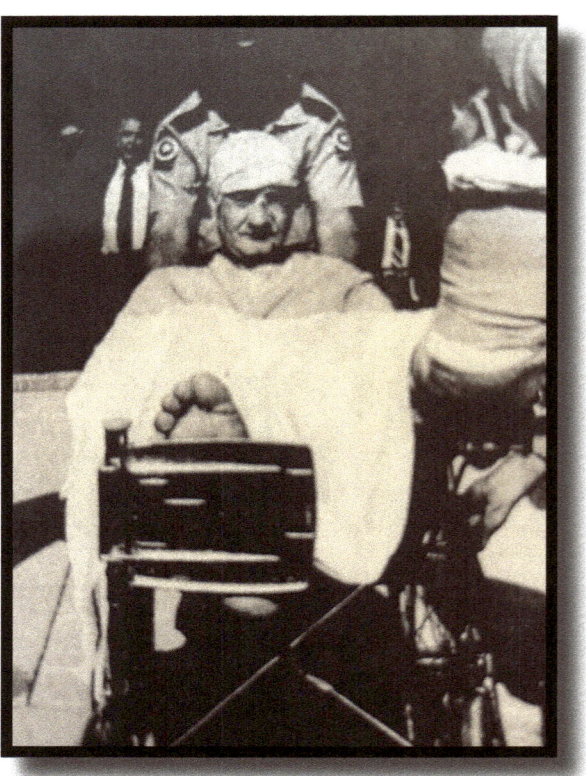

Roy Schultz as he was wheeled into court in Joliet, Illinois, after being released from the hospital.

As the news interview continued, this poor terrorized wife said she had lost the "Good Samaritan philosophy" that prompted she and her husband to stop and render aid. She was then quoted saying "Now, I don't care if you are there with your guts hanging out, I won't stop to help you. No one helped me and I won't help them."

No one could blame the wife who had survived pure evil and complete terror from having those feelings.

For treatment for his injuries, Schultz was taken to a hospital in Peoria, Illinois, and was treated for a severely broken leg, which required surgery. He had multiple near fatal head wounds, which required 158 stitches to suture. After he had healed for eleven days, he was transferred to St. Joseph's Hospital in Bloomington, Illinois, until he was well enough to be booked into jail.

The wife and her daughter were treated in a Bloomington, Illinois, hospital for contusions and stress and later released. This poor wife and mother would later lose her unborn child as a direct result of stress and the physical assault committed against her by Roy Schultz.

The weapons Schultz was in possession of were all stolen from the McGregor Sporting Goods Store. Schultz had once again done nothing to cover his trail of crimes. He was simply a hardened criminal who cared about nothing but himself.

JIM NORTON

CHAPTER 17
Trial Number Two

Roy Schultz was charged with Aggravated Kidnapping/Sexual Assault where it was heard by a jury in Joliet, Illinois. Again Schultz pled not guilty by reason of insanity, and he again asked for and had been granted a change of venue. This case was as widely documented in Illinois newspapers as the 1975 case of the murder of Jerry Ivey in Salina, Kansas.

As a result, the trial was moved from McLean, County to Will County, Illinois. McLean County Attorney Ron Dozier prosecuted the case. The states witnesses included both the husband and wife, police officers, two motel employees, a doctor and others.

Roy Schultz decided to take the stand in his own defense and during his testimony, he began speaking of visions, which "made him want to kill a bad person to make up for his killing of the Kansas police officer." Schultz claimed these visions occurred while he was serving the life sentence in the Lansing, Kansas, prison. Schultz then stated he needed to "cleanse himself," so the person he killed would be accepted by God. It appeared Schultz was trying to sound insane to garner favor with this jury.

It did not work. After only two and a half hours of jury deliberations, the jury returned guilty verdicts for seven counts of aggravated kidnapping, two counts of deviant sexual assault, two counts of taking indecent liberties and one count of armed robbery.

After the trial, Defense Attorney Robert McIntire stated the psychiatrists and psychologist who testified had interpreted their finds differently, which hurt the defense case. Again, they just needed that one box to check on the form.

As a result of Schultz' criminal history and the aggravating circumstances surrounding these heinous crimes, Judge Wayne Townley Jr. (who was probably sickened to his stomach by the details,) sentenced Roy Schultz to between one thousand and fifteen hundred (1,000 and 1,500) years in prison. Yes, you read that correctly. The two counts of deviant sexual assault each brought a 200-year sentence. Judge Townley Jr. had made sure Roy Earl Schultz would never again see life as a free man. And again, it was up to the prison system to ensure it.

The news article depicting this story and prison sentence was printed in the December 23, 1977, edition of the *Effingham Daily News*, from Effingham, Illinois. Needless to say, Schultz had worn out his welcome in Illinois just like he had in Kansas.

Schultz was later transported back to Lansing Correctional Facility in Kansas where he stayed for a couple of years. He would later be transferred to the Missouri State Penitentiary in an interstate prison transfer. Schultz had been moved to a prison in Jefferson City, Missouri.

After the capture of Schultz, (as a direct result of the beating he took at the hands of the husband and wife,) the Salina Police Department and the City of Salina's city commission issued a Proclamation, which was given to this family for their efforts in capturing Roy Earl Schultz. The Proclamation was read aloud at a City Commission meeting on

IVEY BADGE 44

Monday, August 1st, 1977.

The proclamation stated "It is the desire of the Salina community to acknowledge your brave efforts in capturing Roy Earl Schultz, and through the brave and heroic actions by your family, convicted murderer Schultz was apprehended." The proclamation was signed by Salina Mayor Keith Duckers.

The next newsworthy event, which had anything to do with Roy Earl Schultz, occurred on Tuesday, January 3, 1984, when newspapers such as the *Herald* and *Review* in Decatur, Illinois, the *Belleville News Democrat* in Belleville, Illinois, *The Parsons Sun* in Parsons, Kansas, and the *Salina Journal* in Salina, Kansas, reported that at around 2:35 pm, Monday, January 2nd, 1984, a prison guard in Missouri had found Roy Earl Schultz deceased in his prison cell. It is suspected Schultz died of a heart attack at the age of 50. The Monster was no more. The headlines read "Convicted murderer found dead in Missouri prison cell." Schultz had spent just under nine and a half years in prison for killing Officer Jerry Ivey, which included less than seven years of his 1,000-1,500 year sentence for the crimes against the family in Illinois.

Excerpt from the 1975 City of Salina Annual Report, distributed in the form of a wall calendar to the residents of Salina, Kansas.

CHAPTER 18

The Park

There is not a single Police Officer who wears the badge, anywhere in our country, who if asked "would you like a park named after you," would answer "yes." Simply because it would mean it was a memorial park. However, in the case of Jerry Ivey, there is no one more deserving of a park, than he.

In early 1978, the City of Salina had been deeply involved in following up an idea of building a new park to be located in the vicinity of Magnolia and Ohio Streets in south east Salina. Planners had picked a tract of land, they felt would be an ideal location for a new park/green space for citizens to enjoy.

After planning for what seemed like years, the project had finally been digested by the planners, architects, engineers, water department, and parks department and the time was right to start the project.

In July, 1978 ground was broken and the park was beginning to become more than just a passing thought. The park was going to have driving paths or roadways, play grounds equipment for the kids, a duck pond, walking path, covered gazebo, eating areas and a memorial for Officer Jerry Ivey.

In July, 1978, the Salina City Commission had been bound by an earlier order put in place by a previous commission, which banned open parks, green spaces or buildings owned by the City being named after any individual or famous citizens. Personal names for these areas were not permitted.

In early August, 1978, the Salina Parks Advisory Committee had asked the Salina Journal to assist in running a contest to help name the new park. *The Salina Journal* ran advertisements asking citizens to submit their choice to the committee and help "name the park."

On Monday, August 28, 1978, Committee Chairman Dr. David Cole and Mrs. Ann Jett closed the contest and tallied all the entries. It was during this Monday commission meeting they submitted the winning choice to the city commissioners. The winning entry from a total of over ninety submissions was overwhelmingly "Jerry Ivey Memorial Park." Fifteen separate submissions had asked for the park to be named in honor of Officer Jerry Ivey.

Knowing the earlier rule had been put in place years before, the sitting commission decided to change what they felt had been a dumb rule. The commission then closed the open public meeting, went into executive session and voted to change the previous rule. It was during this executive session that the park had been officially named, "Jerry Ivey Memorial Park."

What makes the park special is the actual area set up that memorialize Jerry. It sets along the west side, midway between the north and south ends. When you drive into the west entrance, you face the memorial stone and plaque for Jerry.

In 1979, a ground breaking ceremony occurred and grading, seeding and planting trees commenced. The park is a sprawling 24-acre tract, lined with large overflowing trees of many types. The planners created a mile and a half gravel walking trail around the park that cuts through the beautiful trees. The north end of the park houses two separate playground, including a large rest room facility, a large covered patio and a new water splash area for younger children. A sidewalk runs through the center of the park, from the playgrounds to a large open green area, which, once held the duck pond lined by a concrete wall. The pond was later removed, adding the larger green area for citizens to enjoy. Overlooking the open green area is a huge white wooden gazebo used for ceremonies and family gatherings. A number of weddings have taken place inside the beautiful gazebo. To the south, a winding rock lined sidewalk leads to one of the four covered picnic plazas and the memorial area, honoring Jerry Ivey.

Jerry Ivey Memorial Park Dedication, May 15, 1981. John Burgess, Maryann Ivey with sons, Tony and Jerry Ivey, Jr. and nieces stand in front of bronze plaque in honor of their beloved Jerry Ivey. Photograph Courtesy of the Smoky Hill Museum, Salina Journal Negative Collection.

In the memorial plaza you will find the Jerry Ivey memorial stone and plaque. Two large bushes flank either side of the memorial stone and three, thirty-foot-tall trees enclose the back of the memorial. Donning behind all of that is a tall flag pole with the USA flag flying proudly.

In 1978, when the "name the park" contest was occurring, the Salina Journal decided to give a $250 certificate bond to the winner of the contest. The winner of the contest actually turned out to be the Salina Police Department. As the winner, the police department decided to donate those winning funds to a sculptor, who agreed to create a bronze plaque for Jerry.

Believing the memorial needed something special for the space and for the plaque to be mounted onto, Chief John Woody reached out to his personal friend, Jack Vanier for help. Jack owns a 15,000-acre ranch west of Salina known as CK Ranch. Within the beautiful rolling hills of the ranch, scattered along the hillsides are huge sandstone boulders. With the help of Dale Pike and his wrecker service, a huge sandstone boulder was chosen and Mr. Pike moved the memorial site to where it sits today. It is said that when Mr. Pike drove the stone into the park, the wrecker bed nearly dragged the ground, the boulder was so heavy.

On Friday, May 15, 1981, the Jerry Ivey Memorial Park officially became a city park. A large ceremony was held in the park, dedicating it to all the citizens of Salina in the name of Officer Jerry Ivey. Although Salina has many nice parks open to all people, the Jerry Ivey Memorial Park is special and is enjoyed by citizens on a daily basis. The park will always hold a special place in the law enforcement community, as every year on the third Wednesday of May, police officers, sheriff's deputies, state troopers, fire fighters, citizens and city officials gather to honor all law enforcement officers and first responders lost in the line of duty. The park is a fitting memorial to a hero. If you ever find yourself in Salina, Kansas, may I suggest visiting the park, enjoying a picnic and paying tribute to Jerry Ivey.

Something you might also enjoy knowing, and that may bring a smile, is that on Thursday, June 13, 2024—exactly forty-nine years to the day after Officer Jerry Ivey's passing—a baby girl was born. This little girl, named Millie, is Jerry Ivey's great-granddaughter.

To all who knew him, he was a friend. To all who loved him, they mourned his loss. The death of Jerry Ivey should teach everyone, everywhere, just how devastating an "in the line of duty" death is to a family and their community.

IVEY BADGE 44

North entrance to Jerry Ivey Memorial Park.

Gazebo at Jerry Ivey Memorial Park.

Bronze plaque at Jerry Ivey Memorial Park.

IVEY BADGE 44
SPECIAL THANKS

I wish to give thanks to all the people who helped me in writing the story of Officer Jerry R. Ivey. Your help, information and guidance was invaluable and made this book possible.

I wish to also thank my friend who took his time to act as a beta-reader for this transcript. Andy Meek. Your assistance was truly valuable.

Thank you Jennifer Toelle with Janine Chellington Press for her literary and print publication design knowledge. She did a great job in formatting and publishing my book and creating the cover design. I think it is perfect.

Special thanks to my wife, Amy for proofing the manuscript and for dealing with me while I wrote the book. I am certain I probably drove you crazy. You are awesome. I love you.

This book could not have been written without the permission and oversight from Jerry's sons, Tony Ivey and Jerry Ivey II. Thank you for allowing me to write your dad's story.

And finally, thanks to all you readers who were interested in hearing Jerry's story. I hope if you are ever in Salina, Kansas, you will take the time to visit Jerry's memorial park.

Sources of information:
Ron Styles. Retired Salina Police Department Lieutenant. Ron was a close friend of Jerry and Maryann's and had great detailed memories of his time with Jerry and the SPD. Ron also built the shadow box that hangs in the SPD hallway, containing Jerry's hat badge, name plate and whistle chain.

Jim Huff. Retired Salina Police Department Captain. Jim was instrumental in giving detailed facts about most everything that occurred on that fateful day. Jim was the arresting officer of Roy

Schultz and placed handcuffs on the worst criminal to ever arrived in Salina.

Joe Hay Jr. Current Saline County Commissioner and witness to the death of Jerry Ivey. Joe described in great detail what actually happened at the Triplett station on that fateful day. He witnessed it all and it still affects him.

Darrell Wilson. Retired SPD Assistant Police Chief and retired Sheriff of Saline County, Kansas. Thank you for the story.

Saline County, Kansas, Clerk of the District Court, Teresa Drane and her brilliant staff, for their fantastic court records and document storage system.

Christina Spencer. Current owner of the Ivey home and a very nice lady. Thank you for allowing me to include a photograph of Jerry's family home.

Smoky Hill Museum. For granting photograph rights used in this book.

Rita McLain, Saline County District Court. Rita is the longest tenured Saline County Court employee and her knowledge of the court details are greatly appreciated.

Dana Luoto. Gaston County, North Carolina, school clerk for her help with researching Jerry's school history.

Linda Sikora. Maryann's closest sister and an inspirational lady to talk with. Linda gave great insight into Jerry and Maryann's relationship.

Kansas Law Enforcement Training Center. Thank you for your records regarding Jerry's basic training course attended in 1970.

Angie Fuller. Salina Police Department Records Clerk for answering some needed questions for this stories completion.

IVEY BADGE 44

NEWSPAPERS USED FOR REFERENCE

The Salina Journal, Salina, Kansas.

The Carmi Times, Carmi, Illinois.

The Kansas City Star, Kansas City, Missouri.

The Belleville News-Democrat, Belleville, Illinois.

The Wichita Eagle, Wichita, Kansas.

The Parsons Sun, Parsons, Kansas,.

Herald and Review, Decatur, Illinois.

The Pantagraph, Bloomington, Illinois.

The Argus, Moline, Illinois.

The Decatur Herald, Decatur, Illinois.

The Daily News of Johnson County, Olathe, Kansas.

Freeport Journal-Standard, Freeport, Illinois.

Galesburg Register-Mail, Galesburg, Illinois.

The Daily Republican-Register, Mount Carmel, Illinois.

Effingham Daily News, Effingham, Illinois.

Dixon Evening Telegraph, Dixon, Illinois.

Journal Gazette, Mattoon, Illinois.

Chicago Tribune, Chicago, Illinois.

www.Newspapers.com.

LAST WORDS FROM THE AUTHOR

During my twenty-nine years in law enforcement, I have never heard of a criminal who upended the peacefulness of Kansas, nor who committed as many heinous crimes, or victimized as many people, as Roy Earl Schultz. It is unknown; exactly how many people Schultz killed during his lifetime, however the number of victims he hurt is *mind boggling*.

Interesting Details Learned

While doing research for this book, I learned of the murder of Deputy William Simmons, which occurred in Sangamon County, Illinois, on March 8, 1975. Three months before Officer Jerry Ivey's murder. Roy Schultz was not in jail or prison on March 8, 1975 and the murder occurred in the same county where Schultz grew up, lived and is now buried. Due to the similarities and occurrences involving Roy Schultz both before and after June 13, 1975, it is my personal opinion Roy Schultz was associated with Ronald Edwards, who seventeen years later would be convicted of killing Deputy Simmons. It had been reported Edwards had an "unknown associate" with him just moments prior to the Simmons murder. It is also my opinion during the Simmons murder, the mace canister from Deputy Simmons' patrol car was stolen by Ronald Edwards. I believe Roy Schultz was the "unknown associate" during the Simmons murder and Ronald Edwards was the "unknown associate" with Schultz during the Wichita, Kansas, grocery store robberies on June 10 and 11th, 1975. I also believe it was that same canister of mace stolen from Deputy Simmons, which was used by Schultz to spray Officer Ivey, before shooting him. The connection between Roy Schultz and Ronald Edwards may just be my imagination, however it all seems too coincidental to ignore. I did not intend to inject the Deputy Simmons murder case facts into Jerry Ivey's story, as Jerry's story should stand by itself as a tribute to a very good man. I may investigate further into Deputy Simmons' case to see if it can be connected thorough solid evidence with the Jerry Ivey case.

                                                    Jim Norton
                                                    Gold Badge Writing

ABOUT THE AUTHOR

Jim Norton, a retired police officer with 29 years of experience, is a dedicated true crime writer who conducts his own in-depth research. As the founder of Gold Badge Writing, he brings real-world insight to his storytelling. Jim lives in Salina, Kansas, with his wife, Amy, and their German Shepherd, Hanzo.

To learn more about his work, visit www.goldbadgewriting.com.

You can also reach him at jimnorton@goldbadgewriting.com.

www.ingramcontent.com/pod-product-compliance
Lightning Source LLC
Chambersburg PA
CBHW052032030426
42337CB00027B/4968